HER WORD

A Story of Sexual Assault

IZZY HODDER

Her Word

Copyright © 2021 by Izzy Hodder

All rights reserved.

Published by The Global Edit, the International Division of Red Penguin Books

Bellerose Village, New York

Library of Congress Control Number: 2021913371

ISBN

Print 978-1-63777-103-7 / 978-1-63777-212-6

Digital 978-1-63777-104-4

No part of this book may be reproduced in any form or by any electronic or mechanical means, including information storage and retrieval systems, without written permission from the author, except for the use of brief quotations in a book review.

Contents

A note from the author   xi

Part I
'Her Word'

1. OCTOBER 31ST   3
   - Liv   3
   - Scarlett   11
   - Bee   16

2. NOVEMBER 1ST   23
   - Scarlett   23
   - Ashley (Scarlett's mum)   28
   - Dr. Michaels   34
   - Scarlett   39
   - November 1st: Chris (Sexual Assault Treatment Unit Nurse)   43
   - Samantha   51
   - Suki (Rape Crisis Centre support worker)   57

3. IN ANOTHER VERSION OF THIS LIFE.   71
   - Scarlett   71

4. BEFORE THE TRIAL   81
   - Sam (Garda)   81
   - Kevin Stanley (Scarlett's Prosecution Solicitor)   92
   - Samantha   96
   - David (the accused)   101
   - *Maddy (Scarlett's best friend)*   106
   - Una (David's mother)   111

5. THE TRIAL   119
   - Scarlett   119
   - *Eva (female on the Jury)*   124

6. AWAITING TRIAL RESULTS   131
   - Scarlett   131

7. 2 YEARS LATER   139

8. OCTOBER 31ST 141
What really happened
Epilogue 153

Part II
'Your Word'

'YOUR WORD'	163
Female, 21	164
Female, 21	167
Female, 23	169
Male, 24	171
Male, 24	175
Female, 24	180
Female, 27	188
Female, 23	193
Female, 22	195
Female, 22	196
Female, 23	198
Female, 22	199
Female, 23	202
Female 21	203
Male, 22	204
Female 24	207
Female, 24	207
Female, 22	208
Female, 21	209
Female, 33	209
Female, 22	213
Female, 22	215
Female, 22	215
Female, 20	218
Female, 22	219
Female, 21	222
Female, 24	223
Female, 22	230
Female, 21	230

References	239
Support Services	241
Acknowledgments	243
About the Author	247

This book is dedicated to my huge hearted, inspirational grandmother Angie.
Thank you for teaching me that small acts of kindness are the biggest most important thing we can do for each other.

For everyone, everybody, for all the versions of us out there,
May we always believe. Believe her, believe him, believe each other.
But most of all, believe our-self.

A note from the author

Hi there, firstly thank you so much for seeing this book on a shelf and deciding it was one you would like to read.

Secondly, I want to give an advance warning that there is content in this novel that I do believe all of us can be upset by, but for many of you parts of this novel could be personally hard. So please take your time, if you still do want to read it. And please do know that the content of this novel angers me, which is what motivated me to write it.

I do apologise in advance if anyone finds this telling of a sexual assault case inaccurate, dismissive, wrong, or different in comparison to what they or someone they know went through. And I do feel very strongly that it is so important that I say that. I fully understand that everyone's experience is so different and that 'Her Word' doesn't cover all areas of everything that a sexual assault can involve. There were areas where my knowledge was limited, but like all writers we read and learn and try our best to figure it out. All I can say is that I educated myself as much as I could before every single word.

It is hard to tell any type of story in only one way, so this is just one example. This is only one account of something that has happened to far too many people.

Even if 'Her Word' is completely fictional, the events that happen in this book are more than real for far too many people. But 'Her Word' is a work of fiction.

Scarlett, her friends and family and all the other women and men involved in the fictional part of Her Word are all figments of my imagination.

I would also like to thank the Dublin Rape Crisis Centre for providing services, information and support to the thousands of women and men who avail of their services.

There is a page listing some support services at the back of this novel should you wish to find out more, get support or get involved.

'The most important people to change the world is you. I'm not looking to the government to change my life; I'm not looking toward the next president; I'm not looking toward our next world leaders. I'm looking at everyone in this room. I mean, you are culture.'

~ Lady Gaga

PART I

'Her Word'

1

October 31st

Liv

*'You never know though do you, you keep going until the very last moment…
Because there's always hope… isn't there?'*

'Red cups on the table, beers in the back garden, pizza's on their way….' My mind raced. I had definitely forgotten something. 'What else is there?' I asked my three best friends who were all shuffling around my kitchen, turning on fairy lights and adjusting the same cushions they had adjusted two minutes previously. Placing those tiny useless ornaments that every household collected behind something and then realizing it was probably in a more dangerous spot there so putting it back exactly where they had found it.

'I'm sure it'll be fine' said Maddy un-reassuringly, I rolled my eyes. She shrugged sorry. Bee coughed awkwardly. She didn't even like parties, I was surprised we even had her here tonight.

'It's your first party to host' she said 'no one is going to expect it to be perfect'

Wow, that was even more helpful.

'Remind me again why I call you guys my best friends again?' I asked laughing.

'Because' said Scarlett throwing a cushion in Bee and Maddy's direction 'we are your entourage for what is going to be the best night of everyone who comes to this house's life'

She reached behind her for her bag and pulled out a tiara 'for the princess of the night' she said placing it on top of my head 'and the ultimate host, to you Liv' she raised her arm 'and the best Halloween ever'

'To Liv' smiled Bee and Maddy raising their empty hands, we all noted this and laughed.

'A drink would help I suppose' laughed Maddy

'Come on, let's go get ready. This place is perfect enough' Scarlett pulled our arms in the direction of the stairs. No one else was home, my parents were out of town for the night. It was their anniversary so they'd booked themselves into some nice spa in Wexford and handed me the keys with a knowing look. 'Just be safe Liv and remember, we're only a phone call away' I hugged them goodbye and promised to send them pictures of the girls over later. They were gone less than ten minutes when Maddie came knocking, vodka and lemonade in hand and a big smile on her face.

Now we had set up my home. We just needed to set up ourselves.

'You know, if you're not using this I might actually be a princess tonight?' I said to Scarlett as we made our way up the stairs.

'Oh please do, go for it. It was one of my options but tonight, tonight I think I'm feeling in a more devious mood'

We all rolled our eyes at her 'When are you not darling' said Maddy as we started getting ready in my room.

'Hey now' grinned Scarlett mock punching Maddy. She looked to us all, 'so what are you all going to be then?'

I raised the tiara as an answer,

'I'm thinking of being an angel but like a sexy one….of course' said Maddy

'Omg perfect, I was going to be a devil, we can be a duo!' cried Scarlett. I turned my back and pretended to start painting my nails. I knew I was over sensitive but my gut always felt like Scarlett and Maddy were closer. I knew the same could be said for myself and Bee. But I always felt like the two of them had so much more fun than Bee and I did. Bee was conservative and shy, I loved her so much but a part of me wanted to be wilder and have more fun, the way Scarlett and Maddy did but I always thought Bee would judge me. She was so perfect and good. I never feared judgment from Scarlett, she was the only person I'd told about my summer camp encounter with one of the camp advisors. He was only a year older than me even though he was a camp advisor but I ended up kissing him and we did everything apart from sex one night. Scarlett totally understood what I was feeling when I arrived home all over the place. I knew if I told Bee that she wouldn't say much but I worried that she would think less of me. Or at least I thought she would. But she didn't think less of Scarlett and she knew that Scarlett had sex and did bits all the time but she also knew Scarlett would take no shit if Bee ever said anything. I admired Scarlett for being herself with us. Her actual full self, there was no hidden personalities. I think that must be really hard but I still wish I could do it.

'I think I'll be a bee' said Bee hopping up from my bed and walking over to her bag.

'A bee?' I asked carefully, Bee was very sensitive. Our little worrier, you had to let her down easy if you thought one of her ideas wasn't very…well… thought out.

'Yeah you know; like my name. It'll be very original right' she said before pulling out a huge yellow and black jumpsuit from her bag 'Mum picked it up at a second hand sale yesterday, it fits perfect' she held it out for us to see. It was full legged, full armed black and yellow stripes all the way down. V-necked with a choker at the top. At least that part added a little sauce I suppose.

Maddy coughed, ever the subtle one.

'Well' I started 'a bee is…'

Maddy laughed 'babe a bee is like… –'

But before Maddy could finish her no doubt complimentary opinion Scarlett cut her off.

'A bee… a bee could be a great idea' said Scarlett shooting me and Maddy a look. She walked over to Bee and her costume. 'Is there wings?' she asked

'Yes, they're in here' Bee rooted in her bag and produced a set of massive yellow mesh wings.

'Perfect; we can use these to make hair bands and a bracelet, ooh maybe even some garters'

We all looked at her. Garters. On Bee. I wanted to see that.

'What? It's a good idea, especially since that's your name... good thinking, all the outfit needs is a little adjusting, give me ten minutes and you'll have the best outfit of the night'

'Okay' said Bee, cautiously handing over her jumpsuit and wings reluctantly. Maddy turned on some music and we all started getting ourselves ready to Dua Lipa.

Scarlett was coming in and out of my bedroom with the outfit, scissors and other bits and pieces, we left her to it. Scarlett had a very tough exterior but the softest soul. She would do anything for her friends, people would be here in an hour and she wasn't even dressed but she would more than likely spend the next hour making sure Bee felt beautiful.

'What are you going to be again?' Maddy asked me

'I'll stick with a princess' I said 'the tiara is cute'

'A sexyyyyy princess' shouted Scarlett from the hallway.

'Yes a sexy princess obviously' I shouted back.

Maddy laughed.

'Is Mitch coming?' asked Bee.

'He said he would be but honestly who knows' I said shrugging.

'He better be here' said Maddy 'it's about time you two sealed the deal'

I didn't say anything.

'What is it?' asked Bee. Her intuition was always on.

'I don't know, he's been kind of off lately, all over me one day then he doesn't text back for hours the next' I said, almost too embarrassed to admit this.

Scarlett walked into the room

'Sadly Liv, that is boys and their hormones but in no way is that an excuse to treat you badly, is he worth it?' she asked tilting her head to the left, the scissors dangling from her finger.

They all looked at me, I could feel my face turning red. 'I don't know' I admitted 'you never know though do you, you keep going until the very last moment...because there's always hope....isn't there?' I looked at the girls. Bee was wringing her hands, looking helpless but concerned.

'Oh Liv' she said comfortingly... not knowing what to say next.

Both her and Maddy looked to Scarlett, this was her territory. Somehow over the years of our friendship Scarlett had become the mom of the group when it came to boy troubles.

She always knew what to say, we all had our skills. Bee was a wonderful listener, she also was the first to know if anything was wrong and to quietly ask you what she could do. Maddy could make you laugh until your stomach hurt just when you needed it the most and I, well I was good at being hopeful; at making the girls happy, not in the laughing sense that Maddy was. More in the lets grab every day sort of sense. I'd lost my sister a few years ago to cancer. That's a whole different story but it made me want to live every day as if we weren't guaranteed the next, and to encourage my closest people to do the same.

But when it came to anything boy, love or sex related, Scarlett was our expert. And at this particular time, boys were taking up way too much of our precious brains pace. I hated to admit this but I knew it was true.

Scarlett smiled and sat down next to me.

'Hope is great Liv, trust me we do it all the time right. Hope he will say sorry, hope he make up for it somehow, hope he'll surprise us and make us smile. Hope he'll suggest doing something different for once. But sometimes you've got to protect yourself, not protect yourself so much that you never ever get hurt, but enough so you never get hurt beyond repair. Does that make sense?"

I nodded, I could see where she was coming from. I read enough books to know how broken a person can become given the wrong love, even if I had never experienced this myself. I sort of thought I could guess what it would feel like. Scarlett put her hand on my knee

"Now I don't believe Mitch could ever hurt you beyond repair.... But maybe I'm wrong.... Do you feel, I dunno, right with him?' she asked me

'I guess not. Really I just really thought we had potential' I said

'Yeah I understand, well you know what, maybe give tonight a clean slate, see how it goes and if he's not at least respecting what you're expecting from him then adios' she waved her hand. I laughed.

'What about the rest of you all' I said, attempting to get the attention off me.

'Well' said Maddy blushing

'Omg who who' cried Scarlett pouncing on her as Maddy sat down on my bed.

'Oh stop it's nothing, like really nothing' Maddy said her face attempting to be serious.

'Stop it come one tell us' cried Bee

'Well, I think...I'm not sure but I think that David has been flirting with me a bit in class....we've English together' Maddy blushed when she said his name.

'David Atten?' I asked 'omg please say it's the one who got super-hot over the summer, I swear I didn't even recognize him in his latest posts?'

'Yes yes that David, he's friends with the Josh and Michael crowd you know....I don't know it's probably nothing but I mean he said he was coming tonight....'

'Ah that's so exciting' said Bee 'you should definitely make a move'

By chance I glanced over at Scarlett, simply because she was being unusually quiet. Maddy obviously was thinking the same thing and looked over to her too.

'Well' said Maddy nudging her 'what are thinking missy'

'Maddy' Scarlett gulped 'I really really hate to say this and the only reason I haven't told you guys yet is that this week has been so busy and it completely slipped my mind but....'

'Oh no you've hooked up with him haven't you' cried Maddy putting her face into her hands. Scarlett grimaced and nodded 'I didn't know you were into him I'm so sorry, it was like two weeks ago, we didn't too do much though if that's any help...'

I couldn't keep in my laughter but it was okay because just as I did Maddy burst out laughing too.

'Oh my god, typical' I laughed good naturedly and both Scarlett and Maddy laughed in agreement. Bee looked as though she was in shock, as per usual. She should be used to us by now.

'But I mean he's obviously all yours now darling' laughed Scarlett 'I haven't talked to him since nor do I intend on. And now that I know that you're into him I definitely wont be - but he's nice, he's really nice' Scarlett winked and we all groaned. She laughed 'I'm messing, well I'm not, but you should one hundred percent go for it'

Maddy laughed 'well thank you, I'm glad he got your approval anyways'

Scarlett raised her eyebrows 'Oh honey we have to train them for each other, what goes around comes around' she winked.

We burst out laughing.

'But but.... How?' Bee was shaking her head. Mouth gaping open like a fish.

'Oh Bee, it really doesn't matter. They're boys, we're only young, we may as well share them. Didn't our parents always tell us that sharing is caring' laughed Maddy.

'But does it not make you feel weird?' she asked innocently.

Maddy shrugged, 'not really, it's not like we haven't been with the same guy before'

'Josh' I offered up

'Samuel' said Scarlett

"Alec" Bee couldn't help but add, we laughed.

'The list goes on' agreed Scarlett 'but look Maddy, tonight he is all yours. I can't wait' she clapped her hands together 'oh and Bee…'

Scarlett raced out of the room and returned with a transformed Bee outfit. 'For our sweetest' she said handing it to her. Bee smiled.

'For the first time in my life' she said 'I've got a good feeling about tonight'

Scarlett

'but the truth is I would always forgive him'

I locked the bathroom door behind me and leaned up against it, my body sinking slowly to the floor. I couldn't that believe he was here. It had been months since I'd seen his face, yet he still held a sort of power over me that made my stomach flip with one single glance. I got up off the floor, seriously Scarlett and looked at myself in the mirror. He had changed I thought as I gazed absentmindedly. His hair was longer, his smile smaller. Or maybe it was simply that I just wanted his smile to be smaller… maybe I was searching far too hard for a sign that maybe just maybe I had left an impact on him. That he missed me. That he wasn't quite the same without me. I was looking for something that more than likely didn't exist. I've found before though that far too often our very own memory can be tainted with imagination. We see what we want to see.

I told myself to stop. I tried to convince myself that I didn't have feelings for him. I couldn't still have feelings for him. But it was as futile to think it now, as it had been every time I tried to convince myself I was over him for the last few months. Or should I say years. I put up a good front but I of course I am not a robot. I know I sometimes seem like I'm this inhumane force who doesn't get attached to the boys she sleeps with. And yes, I won't lie, for the most part that's true. But Joel, Joel was my blind spot. Let me tell you a story.

Joel. He was Liv's cousin; which also explained why he was here tonight. Honestly, I can't believe I hadn't thought of it. The first time I met Joel was at Liv's mum and dad's wedding, they got married two years ago. We were all fifteen. Joel was seventeen.

He had that guitar playing, deep thinking look about him. You know the one. The kind that we should all hopefully outgrow but will all want at some point in our life.

All he had to do was glance at me for a second longer than normal and I was already hooked. We danced together, as everyone does at weddings, pretending we were older than we were. Pretending we knew more than we did. Trying to act as if this was something we did all the time. The next day he asked Liv for my number. As you can imagine, that first text I got from him made my stomach flip. He lived near enough to me but went to an all boy's boarding school outside of Dublin. We started seeing each other every weekend and soon enough we were going out. Just like that, we were official. I can't even comprehend how quick and slow it all felt.

He asked me to be his girlfriend at midnight in a playground near my house that we always went to and sat on top of the climbing castle. To me it was the perfect way. In the same way he could have asked me to be his girlfriend in the middle of Penny's and I would have thought that was also perfect. It was simple. He was my first boyfriend. My first significant person. The only boy I had ever cared about. We never had sex. It was just after him that I had sex with a guy I had grown up with at a party. It was a rebound but I suppose it was also slightly out of spite. I knew Joel had really wanted to have sex. Joel; well all the girls will tell you Joel was a dickhead. Even before we started dating Liv warned me that he had a reputation with girls. He was a good guy, sure he was sweet and nice, but he was a player. As Liv whispered to me, 'he thought with his…' she then pointed downwards. I had laughed at the time but five months into going out I unfortunately discovered it was true. He cheated on me, he had sex with another girl at a party. I had been sick and couldn't go out that night. He told me straight away, that very night and he broke up with me. Over the phone at 2am. He was cruel and awful and he told me he needed sex but knew I wasn't ready for it. He said these exact words, words I fear I'll never forget "sorry but I can't keep going with you without it" I almost got sick on my front porch the next morning when he called over to give me back a bracelet. But when he walked away... I won't say it broke something in me because it felt more like something had been taken out of me, something so engrained in my body that I felt empty without it. As if a vital part of my functioning body was suddenly removed and I could no longer work properly without it.

I pretend to be strong, of course I do it's how I am. Isn't it how we all are. I pretend to be invincible but the truth is, I would always forgive him. And if he ever wanted to, as ashamed as I am to admit this, I would take him back in an instant.

I blinked at myself in the mirror. Attempting to remove myself from the irretrievable past, I tucked my hair behind my ears and looked closely at myself in the mirror. It might sound crazy but I spoke to myself. This was a long time habit of mine.

'Don't you dare let him back in' I said over and over until I laughed and sighed. Maddy called it blind spots, the way I felt about Joel. She would say that there's some people we will always have blind spots for, only see the good parts of them; and it's dangerous because in doing so we ignore who they really are. We ignore the bad because we don't want it to exist. Joel was my blind spot, no matter what he did I would always see some more good in him.

'Get it together' I told myself sternly this time. I straightened down my little red velvet skirt. I spotted a bottle of wine opened on the bathroom shelves, left precariously on the edge between Liv's bottles of OGX shampoo. I made a mental note to tell her what I had read recently about them being bad for your hair.

Liv and Bee had been in here getting ready, they must have left that bottle of wine behind. I wasn't much of a drinker, many a night I went out and didn't take a sip while everyone around me drank away. It wasn't because I thought I didn't need it, it was more I just hadn't found a drink I actually enjoyed drinking yet, and I usually ended up with a tummy ache for at least a day or two after. I didn't find it worth it.

But tonight, tonight that bottle of wine looked like fun, it looked like a distraction. It looked like it opened up a side to me that I didn't know very well yet. I grabbed it. Almost full…great I thought taking a big slug.

'You've got this' I told myself one last time in the mirror before turning away and opening the bathroom door, stepping out onto the landing. Wine bottle and feigned self confidence in hand.

By the time I reached the bottom of the stairs all that self-confidence was gone and I was making me way steadily and far too quickly through the bottle.

'Scarlett' Bee walked up to me where I was standing by myself underneath the stairwell.

'Hey' I smiled at her 'You look great' I said enthusiastically, looking at her much improved bee outfit. I stepped towards her and stumbled a little. She grabbed my arm to stop me from swaying. I had definitely drunk that far too quickly. It had gone straight to my head.

'You alright darling?' she asked, looking concerned.

I nodded slowly. I was looking around me, half hoping I would see him, half hoping I wouldn't. not knowing how I would react to either result. My heart was literally racing.

'A lot of people just arrived at once…'said Bee, smiling but looking nervous. Shifting ever so slightly from foot to foot. Social situations just weren't her comfortable place. I wrapped my left arm around her.

'That's so good, I feel like we always worry but then end up wishing that so many hadn't come...hey lets' go get some more drinks, see what everyone's up to' I said as I took another sip. Bee nodded and smiled 'sure, come on' but she looked at me curiously. Nevertheless, she didn't question, she knew something was up but she let me lead her into the kitchen towards the buzz of people and the loud music. She held me tightly. I squeezed back and there in the corner I saw him again. Sipping his beer, by himself. I froze. My throat tightened. Why is it some people affect us in such a way that the energy in a room literally shifts once they are in it.

'Scarlett come on, want to find the other girls?' said Bee tugging on me to keep hold of me amongst all the people. It really was getting crowded in here.

'Ehm....'I hesitated but then I was overcome with this strong sense of why not. Why not go up to Joel and talk to him. That's all, just talk. We could be friends couldn't we? Had it not been long enough. My courage (and the wine making its way through my body) grew until it seemed to me so absolutely unreasonable to do anything but go and talk to him.

'Bee I'm just going to go talk to Joel' I said simply.

'Wait Scarlett...' Bee looked where I was looking and clocked him there. She sighed 'are you sure?' was all she asked.

I nodded quickly and gulped back the last of the bottle of wine. That had gone far too quickly, there had probably only been a small bit left, 'Of course, I just want to see how... I want to see how he's.... see how he's doing, it's been a while'

Bee nodded and let go of my hand slowly. I turned away. I placed the empty bottle on a nearby table and I looked straight ahead. Joel lifted his head. His Adam's apple bulging as he gulped down the beer. He looked right back at me.

Bee

"It was almost as though she were afraid to feel love. For fear it wasn't there"

I snuck behind the living room door, from here I had a clear view of Scarlett and Joel talking over in the corner. Just in case anything looked like it was going wrong. I took out my phone and pretended to be replying to texts. If anyone noticed me they would know I was bluffing, they would know I was the awkward one, because who the hell ever texted me apart from Liv, Maddy or Scarlett. But that was one of the pros of being nothing much, not that pretty, not that funny, not that smart, people didn't really notice me. If I was there or not, what I was doing, or who I was doing it with. To this day I'm still not sure how I ended up with the friends that I have, there was probably a blip in the system on the day we all meet. Surely someone who looked like me, watched Doctor Who and who read books about microbiology purely for the fun of it; surely I should have ended up sitting alone in the library every lunch time. However, here I was, at a party, one I didn't actually feel too uncomfortable being at. And sure, maybe my main job at this party was to look out for my friends, and yes I suppose I did give that job to myself but I couldn't help it. It's where I felt more comfortable. I was worried about Scarlett. I knew Joel had hurt her so much more than she would ever let on, I may not be as close to her as Maddy but I clearly remember this one night. It was about six months after Joel broke up with her, Scarlett called me at two am. I was still awake, I was one of those people who found reading just as restful as sleep and was nearly always half-awake with my night light on and my book on the planets lounging on my stomach.

'Bee' said a shaky voice that would have hardly recognized as hers.

'Scarlett' I sat up in my bed 'Are you okay? What's wrong?'

'Bee…. I'm outside' she said sobbing

'Outside where, what do you mean? Outside my house?' I sprung up, my book dropping to the floor with a thump, and walked to my window but there was no one out there.

'No, no don't worry… I'm outside my own house…' the wind howled in the background 'well actually I'm just….I'm kind of just wandering around near mine….it's so peaceful at this time' her voice was wistful.

'Scarlett please go home, or I can come and meet you' I said thinking of how alone she was. How dark it was. How empty the streets around her house were.

'No …no' she replied softly.

'What's wrong honey….' I knew what was wrong but I wasn't expecting her to admit it. Scarlett never admitted it.

'He didn't want me Bee' she took a deep breath to steady her voice. 'It feels like I woke up and he was gone….it feels like a bad dream that I can't seem to wake up from ….that I won't ever wake up from….'

For a mere moment I was speechless. I mean Scarlett never looked for help, she was Scarlett. She always appeared unbreakable, strong, the one we all turned to for advice. The one who didn't let outside sources affect her own self, her own mood and thoughts. The one who seemed unphased by anything life would throw her way. When her and Joel broke up, the very next day she shrugged her shoulders at us in assembly and said, 'A boy needs to be able to do more than play guitar anyways, and what kind of an age is this to commit, the more the merrier' she had then progressed to organise a girls spa night for us all. At which I think Joel was mentioned twice and we spoke more about my most recent grades and Maddy's recent fight with her parents. Scarlett was not a dweller, or at least she didn't let on she was.

That night however, Scarlett was still breathing down the phone…'I just mean…it's made me doubt everything I thought I knew… everyone I thought I could rely on…couldn't they just leave me the way he left me? Without notice, without a goodbye….what's to stop people from leaving? And how can I prepare for it when they will'

'Oh no Scarlett, that's'….' I thought of what I should say, what did I know to say….had I ever been left? No, I had never even been in a position in which someone could actually leave me. I didn't know what to say but I spoke - 'Scarlett that's not true. You, you were amazing, you are amazing, and you know it. Or if you don't, you should know it. He just didn't see it, he left the best thing he probably ever found, and you know what, the next boy who gets you will feel so lucky that Joel let go of what he will then have' Okay I know it was a weird angle to take on it, but I was stuck. I wasn't used to this. I had never had to support a friend through this, I had never felt anything remotely like this before either.

Scarlett sobbed 'It's okay…I know I don't need anyone….none of us do, but thanks Bee'

'Will you go home now?' I asked concerned as I hopped back into my bed.

'Yeah, I'm on my way…. goodnight Bee'

'You'll be okay Scarlett' I said softly

'Bee please don't say this to anyone else okay' Scarlett asked, suddenly serious.

'Of course not….' I lay back down.

'Okay bye, I love you' Scarlett hung up straight away, not even giving me the chance to say it back. But maybe she preferred it that way, Scarlett gave love so freely and overwhelmingly. Yet she rarely allowed it to be returned.

Back here and now at the party, I looked up from my phone to where she stood touching Joel's arm, he now had his arm around her back. I thought again, she gave love freely but never expected any of it back…. If you tried to be kind to her you were returned with a joke. A rolling of the eyes. It was almost as though she were afraid to feel love. For fear it wouldn't be there. I wondered if this was always the way she had been. Or had she accidentally developed this trait without even realizing. When I thought about it I had only really known the recent versions of Scarlett, we had all met when we were thirteen but really we probably only grew into our selves by the age of fifteen. Only let ourselves being more seen as we felt more secure with each other. And although we felt as tight as a group of friends could be, that was only a few years of life together. How much could we really know about the people we once were or would become.

But right now I was worried of how easily Scarlett would fall back into the trap of Joel's smile. He was whispering something in her ear and taking her hand in his. I put my phone into the strap of my skirt and walked towards them. They were headed towards the kitchen counter. Scarlett shakily poured herself another drink and then dropped the glass the minute she picked it up. A loud crash as it shattered against the floor caused everyone to look at her.

'Ooopsie' she giggled, very obviously drunk but still looking like a natural superstar. You could almost see grateful look on all the guys face's that they had an excuse to stare at her for a moment in her little red outfit.

I raced over to her

'Don't move' I said 'there's glass everywhere'

'Here I'll grab the brush' said Joel, ducking into the utility room. I took the chance to speak to Scarlett.

'Are you okay with him?' I asked quietly, moving her carefully away from all the broken glass.

She smiled happily and kissed me on the cheek 'More than okay, never better'

I gave her a squeeze as she nestled her head onto my shoulder giving me a kiss. Joel returned with the dustpan and brush. Scarlett was happy, I couldn't be the protective mother when she didn't want me to be. I shouldn't.

I lifted Scarlett's head off my shoulder and Joel wrapped his arm around her.

'I'll clean this up' I said and smiled at Scarlett who gave me a grateful smile back. followed by a wink. So Scarlett.

'Cheers Bee that's really good of you, have a great night' they turned around and headed into the hall. I started to sweep up the chunky shards of sparkling glass. When I looked out into the hall, they were walking up the stairs. Scarlett was stumbling and giggling, Joel was pulling her up. I placed all the broken glass into a bag and threw it in the bin.

2

November 1st

Scarlett

*'All I wanted to be was who I was before I remembered.
But forgetting isn't a choice'*

I woke up with a start. The kind of waking that makes you jump in your bed. I was confused. It was dark wherever I was. Where was I? I automatically reached out my hand in the hope of it coming across my phone. But instead my hand rested upon something soft, a teddy. I squinted to make it out. Not my teddy, no, it was Liv's. I was in Liv's bed. Joel….his hand. My mind raced and I jolted upright. But I moved too quickly and suddenly a wave of nausea hit me and I leaned over the bed and started to retch. The door opened. The light was so bright beaming in and for some reason I let out a tiny scream. Darkness was in my head. I couldn't remember, but it hurt. Something hurt. There was a knot in my stomach.

'There you are, is there anyone else in here?' It was Bee. I'd never been so happy to hear her voice. A familiar voice. But why was she asking was there anyone else in here? Why would she ask that? I turned my head nervously, suddenly feeling like there was someone next to me, too close to me…. On top of me. I shook my head. What was going on.

I tried to speak 'Bee, no, no one else is here…Bee what happened…what-'

I started to get sick. Properly sick this time. Bee turned on the lights in the room and raced over.

'oh dear, Liv is going to kill you, here come with me to the bathroom,'

The bathroom. I heard a crack, in my memory, there was something there. Hiding. It wasn't nice. But my head hurt too much to think about it. It felt all musty. And where had Joel gone? Did I just imagine that he had been here? Did I dream it? I wouldn't put it past me, he was always appearing in my dreams. I let Bee help me out of bed. She led me out onto the landing and into the bathroom. It was even brighter in here.

'Here sit down' said Bee. I didn't want to sit on tiles. Why didn't I want to? I felt like I was moving through motions without properly being present. I didn't feel inside my body.

'I need to pee' I said abruptly, my mind flashing with images. How much had I drunk? Was I still dreaming? Something about everything felt off. Felt very off.

I sat down on the toilet and then almost screamed out in pain. Bee looked up from the sink panicked.

'What's wrong, what's wrong? Oh no did you have sex with Joel and forget to pee afterwards? Scarlett you're always telling us to never do that! Have you gotten an UTI?'

'What?' had I slept with Joel? I remembered, or I thought I remembered me and him in Liv's bed but nothing more? That wasn't a dream I knew that now.

'You and Joel, you went upstairs with him last night?'

'I.... I don't know....' I was confused. I was so confused.

Someone banged on the door 'Come on girls, we need to get going home before Liv's parents get back' said Maddy banging on the door. Why did that feel strange. The banging on the door.

Loud noise.

Suddenly there it all was.

I remembered it perfectly.

The moment I did, I wished I had never had. The images hit me, the sounds were suddenly with me. I felt it. I wished I could unfeel it. I could feel David, on top of me. I could remember me trying to get away. I wanted to forget it all. All I wanted to be was who I was before I remembered. But forgetting isn't a choice.

Bee opened the door to Maddy. I was still sitting on the toilet.

'Jeez you look a mess' said Maddy coldly from the doorway, looking me up and down.

'Gotta...go...home' I said shakily, I got up off the toilet. I glanced down. I was in an old oversized t-shirt of Liv's with just my underwear on underneath, but there were stains. Red stains, on my upper leg. I pulled the t-shirt down lower, moving awkwardly. The girls looked at me. I needed to get out of this house. Of this bathroom. Of my body.

'I'm going to call my mum' I said

'I found your phone's downstairs, I think it's dead' said Maddy, her own phone starting to vibrate in her hand.

'Hello, hey mum' she said moving out of the door-way, so I could pass her, my hands self-consciously covering my legs. I realized I was limping to avoid pain.

'Yep she's here with me' she paused and sighed 'No she's fine' Maddy looked me up and down again, I swear she almost rolled her eyes. 'sure I'll ask her…' she said into the phone, she took it away from her ear.

'Mum wants to know if you want a lift home, she said your mums been calling her cause you wouldn't pick up' Maddy's tone was harsh and her eyes wouldn't look directly into mine. But I didn't have the energy in me to worry about why she was acting like this with me. I needed to get home. Or away. Away sounded good.

I nodded 'That would be great thanks'

'Okay see you in a few mum thanks, bye bye bye' Maddy hung up the phone.

'Well you better put on some pants or something, I'll go back down and help Liv' she walked past me in the landing. Bee looked confused. She hated conflict. I could tell she was feeling torn, trying to quickly figure out who would be least mad at her if she went with either one of us.

'Here I'll help you get some clothes' she then said and went back into Liv's room, the smell of my vomit was wafting out of the room. I retched. Bee threw me out a pair of tracksuits, 'these will do, and take my jumper' she took off her own baby pink fluffy jumper and put it on the bed for me as I pulled on the pants. Trying to hide my legs.

'Scarlett….'

I looked at her, I was afraid of what she was going to ask. Or maybe I was afraid of what she wouldn't ask? Afraid of what I would have to say. Or not say. I didn't know which option was worse that than the other.

'Are you okay?' she looked down as she asked the question. I wanted to say no, that no I am not okay but who the hell ever says that when someone asks them. When people ask how you are they never expect to hear the real truth. Maybe I should tell her, I shouldn't hide it right. What was I hiding? But before I could speak - she did 'You're just super hungover right?' and there it was, such a simple human habit that we probably don't even realize that we do it every single day.....people are afraid of the truth. Of the dark truth. Its engrained in us, we want to help, until we realize what help are we. And can we handle the truth? Can we make the truth better. We want the problems to be things we can fix, issues we can fix easily and with words or actions. But when we feel there might not be a quick fix, we put a different problem in its place, a problem we can fix. A hangover.

I nodded, Bee was kind. She was a soft, loving human but she wasn't built for battles.

'I shouldn't have drunk so much' I said, 'thanks for helping me' I gave her a hug. But her body felt weird on mine and I pulled out quickly. 'I better clean up that sick' I said quickly, I grabbed an old towel from the bathroom. There wasn't much and I dropped the towel into the laundry on the landing. Bee was still standing there. Pretending she wasn't watching me.

'Scarlett come on my mums here' Maddy's voice boomed up the stairs. I made my way down them, meeting Liv in the hall.

'Jeez Scarlett you don't look great' she said bluntly. I tried a weak smile and pointed to my head. Hoping that indicated that it hurt. Hoping that it indicated that a hangover was the worst of my worries.

She nodded 'okay well I'll talk to you later' she gave me a quick hug, looking briefly at Maddy as she did so. Was I missing something here? I definitely was, this was not what my best friends were like.

'Here's your phone' said Liv handing me my dead iPhone. I pocketed it.

'Thanks so much for the party' I smiled and followed Maddy out the door and into her car.

On the car ride home, we were all quiet. My head pounded too much for me to even attempt conversations, every time I felt like starting a sentence I couldn't think of how it would end. My thoughts felt like sand slipping through my fingers. Gone before I could fully comprehend what they were. When we pulled up outside my house I thanked Maddy's mum, I looked to Maddy 'See you tomorrow?' I asked, hoping she was just tired.

'We're going away remember' said Maddy, looking ahead at the street and not back at me. Her mum looked at her, giving her a quizzical smile and a gentle nudge. When Maddy didn't react in any way she looked to me and smiled. 'We're going on holidays honey…' of course I remembered. Maddy's family were going to London for the week. It was mid-term.

'God, sorry I completely forgot' I smiled 'have a great time, I'll text you' Maddy nodded and I shut the door. Her mum gave me a confused smile and drove off. I turned around. My mum was already at my front door, holding it open. She did not look happy. I put one foot in front of the other. Looking down at the ground. I had no idea what I was to do from here on out.

Ashley (Scarlett's mum)

'Is it terrible or natural that my first reaction was disbelief?'

When Scarlett walked down the stairs on that first day in November I was angry with her. Earlier when she had arrived home I had been relieved to see my daughter in one piece, which may be irrational when she had only been at her friend's house close by but I think a mother is always glad to see her children in one piece. It was not a thought I would have ever imagined crossing my mind before I became a mother but now I even breathed a sigh of relief whenever her and her sister walked in the door from school.

But because the relief had now passed, I had time to get a little angry. Scarlett had been dropped home completely hung-over from her friend Liv's. I knew there had been a party at Liv's for Halloween night but when I saw the state of Scarlett that morning I was disappointed. Disappointed I guess because I had thought I had raised a child who didn't wake up looking quite as shook as she had that morning. Critical, I know, given I had definitely spent the majority of my twenties looking exactly like that. But isn't it normal to not want to pass quite everything on to our children, to only give them the glittery good parts of ourselves. Of course, I was also worried, Scarlett usually text me to let me know how she was or at least always replied to my messages but not that night. My worry turned to anger when I saw her hungover but at least alive and in one piece.

So as I was standing there washing dishes with my younger daughter Samantha, you can imagine I didn't have the biggest smile for my eldest daughter when she walked into the kitchen.

'Mum' she said, her voice quiet. Coming to apologize I presumed as I continued to put away plates.

'Yes Scarlett' I said briskly handing Samantha a plate to dry. She kept her head down.

'I think we need to go to the hospital' said Scarlett, staying standing in the doorway. I looked up at her; she was in her jacket and had a bobble hat on. I shook my head and sighed.

'Oh for god's sake Scarlett, where do you think you're going?' I snapped 'you're hung-over, you're bound to feel sick. Stop being dramatic, there's dinner in the oven you'll feel better after getting some food into you'

'No mum' her voice was adamant. I had turned back around to my dishes. Samantha nudged me 'Mom' she said softly.

'What!' I turned back around to look at Scarlett still standing in the doorway. A tear was sliding down her face.

'Scarlett, what's wrong' I took a deep breath 'look don't worry I'm not really mad, we can just talk about –'

'Mum' she was shaking, I took a step towards her but she put out her hand as if telling me to stay away.

'We, we need to go to the hospital'

'What happened, are you okay' my mind began to race. What had she hurt, who had hurt her.

Scarlett shook her head 'something happened' she said steadily her eyes glued to not the floor, but the high ceiling above our heads.

'What, what do you mean? What happened?' my heart pounded.

'Last night, at the party, at Liv's' she looked ahead briefly, eyes darting from me to Samantha.

'Yes, what about the party Scarlett?' I put my hand on the kitchen counter to steady myself.

'Well something.... Something happened'

She paused and took a deep breath, looking at the floor as she spoke

'Mum I was, I was, someone had… sex with me…but I…I didn't want to. I wasn't…. I didn't…I didn't want it to happen'

Is it terrible or natural that my first reaction was disbelief. My first reaction was disbelief, and it wasn't this because I had ever doubted a word my daughter said, no my first reaction was disbelief because I so badly wanted for what Scarlett had just said to not be true. How could I not, of course I didn't want to believe my daughter had experienced something so terrible, so violent. I didn't want to believe I had let this happen to her. I hadn't been there. Wasn't that my one job. To always be there.

'Scarlett, honey what, what happened' I choked out, hating my choice of words even as they were leaving my mouth. I shouldn't be so questioning. I should do what she wants.

Samantha covered her mouth and moved towards her sister.

'I don't want to…I don't want to tell you right now' Scarlett said 'I'm sorry mum, I just want to go'

'Scarlett don't be sorry, is this what you want to do? Go to the hospital, will we talk about it more' a tear rolled down my face. I didn't want to believe her, simple as, but I couldn't deny the truth any longer.

'Mum shh, listen to Scarlett' snapped Samantha standing opposite her sister.

'I'm sorry Scarlett, oh Scarlett I'm so sorry' I walked towards Scarlett but she turned away from me and spoke

'I think we should go. I've got the car keys, Samantha you're coming too'

• • •

Our nearest hospital was about half an hour drive away. Scarlett sat in the front next to me.

'Scarlett…' my voice trailed off, what was I supposed to say. I was her mother I was meant to always know what to say. I was meant to be able to tell her how to deal with things, but I had never dealt with this. This wasn't how life was meant to work, I was supposed to go through all the bad stuff first and attempt to make it easier for her. Know what eased it, what made the bad times a little more bearable. I was supposed to be the example that stuff could happen but you would always be okay. But now, now I had no idea. A friend of mine had been assaulted when we were in college, thinking about it now I knew a few of my friends or friends of friends who had. But we had never done anything and it wasn't really something we liked to discuss that often, I always thought they handled it really well but maybe it was just that we didn't create a safe enough space for them to outlet what they were really feeling. This sounds awful but in my twenties it didn't seem abnormal to hear of something like this happening to a friend. Not overly common but let's just say we weren't shocked. We knew what boys were like.

This was different, I don't know why. I know the impact was the same but I wasn't twenty anymore and this was my daughter. My baby. My complete responsibility.

'Mum should we call dad?' asked Samantha from the back seat, looking from me to Scarlett who after a brief moment, nodded her head slowly.

'I don't want him to know' she said quietly, "I wish no one did".

I pursed my lips, trying to hold in tears. Tim would kill whoever did this to our daughter. I very literally mean kill. He was a tolerant man, a forgiving man but in his line of work he had seen his fair share of horrific people and the last place he ever wanted to imagine them was near either of our daughters.

'Samantha get my phone out of my bag and send your father a text, tell him we're on our way to the hospital because Scarlett's been.....'

Scarlett looked to me, her eyes testing but teary. She was challenging me, but this time it was different because this time we weren't sitting around our kitchen table with her telling us how unisex toilets need to be every-where so people feel more comfortable or how she doesn't care how people ended up homeless, it's what they are now so we deal with what they are not what they could have been. It wasn't theoretical, it wasn't observing the case on the news of sexual assault and having Scarlett ask us all our opinions...it wasn't what we thought should happen. It wasn't just words or intentions. This time it mattered deeply what we said. This time it was her, it was her experience.

The fire in her wasn't as fully there, she was closed down. I knew this wall she built up when things happened to her. She was the same when her grandma died a few years ago, they were so close and when she passed Scarlett shut off from everyone.

'Tell him that something has happened to Scarlett, she's fine but we are going to the rotunda, tell him to meet us there'

Samantha tapped away on my phone obediently.

'Fine' said Scarlett laughing sarcastically

'I'm sorry honey, we can figure out the rest later but he is your dad. And I don't want to scare him on his way to the hospital. He loves you so much.' I cursed myself silently for handling the situation so badly. I was a fucking social worker for god's sake. I took a breath, this wasn't about me. This was about Scarlett.

'Scarlett, before we arrive; do you want to tell me what happened? Whatever it was you can tell me everything I promise'

She shook her head 'I'll tell the doctors or nurses when we get there. I'll tell whoever will fix it, but right now' she started to cry 'right now if I tell you what happened it will make it even more true…..' she gulped 'so I'm going to wait okay, to pretend it isn't so real, for just a few more moments'

Samantha reached out to her from behind and gently took her sisters hand.

'Dad said he would meet us there, at the Rotunda…' she said softly.

Scarlett nodded next to me.

'Okay let's not talk until we arrive…. Let's not….'

Silence came over the car and I kept my eyes glued to the road. I concentrated greatly on every turn, every roundabout, every stop sign. Next to me my daughter shook in her seat. A tear slid down my face. I passed out three cars who were going too slow. I indicated left and pulled into the hospital car park, I parked the car quickly, perfectly and precisely. It was all I could do.

Dr. Michaels

'I knew because we pretend not to know'

I had only been working in the Rotunda hospital for two weeks when Scarlett Love walked in to my consultation room. She was my very first sexual assault patient. That I knew of. I am sure plenty patients I had had been assaulted but had just chosen not to disclose this information.

I had just moved to Ireland from New Zealand. Scarlett was a gorgeous girl...she reminded me of my younger sister back in New Zealand. I thought her name was really pretty. Strong, it stood out. I thought about telling it to my husband it that night, we were trying to have our first child.

When Scarlett walked into my room that afternoon after waiting in the A&E, I didn't know she had been assaulted. She hadn't said it at reception, I can completely understand why but in a way I wish she had. Because then I could have transferred her quicker to the sexual assault unit that we have. The people there were so much better versed in how to deal with these cases.

Scarlett walked into my patient room, followed by a tall, attractive looking woman I presumed to be her mum. I stood up to shake her hand and introduce myself.

'Hi, I'm Dr. Michaels, please take a seat' I sat back down as Scarlett and her mum sat opposite me. Straight away I noted an air of awkwardness. I thought maybe Scarlett was here to talk about a UTI or STD and that's why she felt awkward with her mum also being there.

'How can I help you today Scarlett?'

Silence.

I looked from Scarlett to her mother. Both were wringing their hands identically and looking at their laps. 'Scarlett would you prefer if we had this consultation alone?' I asked. She was old enough. Her mother's presence didn't seem to be helping the situation right now.

Scarlett nodded; her mother's face flashed the briefest look of relief before being quickly replaced with one of worry.

'Scarlett are you sure? I won't...' her voice trailed off.

Scarlett looked up at her 'I'll be okay mom'

Her mum looked at me pointedly, as if pleading with me silently to make her daughter better. I got a knot in my stomach. I didn't know what Scarlett was here for, but my gut was telling me that I was going to remember this patient.

Once her mum had closed the door gently behind her, Scarlett rose her head and cleared her throat.

'Last night..' she started, and I knew. I immediately knew.

Why? How did I know?

I knew because I've heard those words before.

I knew because hadn't so many women, mothers, aunties, sisters, friends heard them too?

I knew because we all know too many people.

I knew because we pretend not to know.

I knew because it was always there. Always hidden away yet always right in front of us.

Scarlets voice broke 'Last night, someone, he did something to me'

I nodded and thought carefully before I spoke.

'Scarlett, would you like to tell me what he did?'

'He had sex with me, I…. I was very drunk. I'm not…. I don't know if that means…anyways I was drunk, I was asleep. I don't remember it well…I tried to stop it'

'I'm really sorry this has happened to you Scarlett' I said softly

A tear slid down her cheek, she wiped it away quickly, looking down into her lap. I handed her a tissue.

'Me too' she said 'I don't know what to do' she looked at me.

I so badly wanted to take it all away for her. Make her forget. That's what I wished I could do.

'This is a trauma to the body Scarlett, so it's only natural to feel confused. Would you like me to tell you about a few of the options you have as of right now?' I hated how clinical I sounded but I tried to remember that this was not about me. And that I was trained to offer solutions, even if none would or could suffice.

Scarlett just nodded. Her eyes dry now.

I tried to keep my facial expression neutral but for some reason I felt such anger. I didn't know this girl, but I couldn't bear that she and so many other women went through this and that we didn't do anything. We as a species and we as humans, as me and you.

I was here, I was a doctor I was supposed to help and fix and heal. But you can't help and fix and heal this with anything medical. Do we even have anything that can heal this?

'Dr. Michaels' asked Scarlett before I was about to tell her the different options. She looked nervous.

'Do people come here when this kind of thing happens? I didn't know what to do.....but is this normal?' her eyes were sort of pleading with me, silent asking me to tell her that she wasn't alone in this. And as awful as it is, she is not alone in this. It unites far too many people.

I thought of my time in college studying medicine and how I had taken a volunteering module and for it I worked in a woman's crisis centre, there was a lot of domestic violence, neglect, money problems, but one thing they nearly almost all had in common. Some kind of sexual abuse. It had terrified me how common it was. It almost came hand in hand with being born a female, you were just lucky if you went through your whole life without experiencing it. Scarlett was not alone, even if she felt it. And throughout my time there I couldn't help but think that it really is used as one of the most powerful ways of controlling women. By instilling a fear in us that we cannot do certain things because it is too dangerous and then encouraging the fact that we need another man to protect us from the bad men. It is always men in the position of power. We are still not able to do as much as them, we are still told to be more careful constantly, we are still told no, don't do that, don't go there, definitely not alone, definitely not without a man. We are still told watch yourself and not throw yourself into it. I believe it is an underlying way of keeping us in our box. It is a million times harder to achieve your goals when walking home from work every night can still instill a huge amount of fear.

'To tell you the truth Scarlett, I have not been at this hospital long so I have not had many encounters here…but I worked in New Zealand before and I'll tell you one thing. It's everywhere, worldwide I think the figure is 35% of women have experience this. The UN says the figure worldwide is 1 in 3 women.'

Scarlett nodded 'it's weird but that kind of helps, as terrible as it is' she looked down. 'what am I supposed to do now? Her voice quivered and I wanted to wrap this young, gorgeous, heartbroken girl up in my arms.

'Well Scarlett it is completely up to you as to how you want to….deal with this, or go forward with this. Here in the hospital we have a unit specially dedicated to victims of sexual assault, so I could bring you over there and they could talk you through your options a bit more? I'm so sorry that there's not more I can do but the nurses and specialist over there know a lot more than me….what do you think?'

Scarlett was looking at me, she attempted a small smile and nodded. I stood up and smiled softly at her, I headed towards the door and she followed.

That was my encounter with Scarlett Love. That is all the time I had with her and I feel as though I will never forget a second of it.

As I was opening the door for Scarlett I was thinking to myself, that, for me this experience lasts approximately 10 minutes. For Scarlett, this very well may last her whole life.

Scarlett

'That seemed like a tempting but dangerous option. To not feel. Feeling was all I knew. Feeling was all we had.'

The doctor, she was so nice but I felt like everyone was suddenly scared of me. I wanted it to all stop. I wished I hadn't told anyone. Why did I even open my mouth. Why the hell did I think it was a good idea to come to the hospital. It did hurt, yes, but maybe it would go away. Actually my head really hurt, the back of my head. I should tell someone that. Something felt very off in my whole body but maybe I was hungover, maybe it too would go away. Maybe if I ignored everything it would eventually all go away. Hadn't that always been Liv's attitude 'ignore it and it will go away' we always made fun of her for it, telling her that our Leaving Cert was not just going to go away, neither was our lack of having any idea of who to invite to our debs. I wished her saying worked a lot right now.

I saw my dad sitting with my mum and Samantha when Dr. Michaels walked me out of her room and my stomach flipped. I hated this. I hated this. I hated this. I wondered for a moment, had I been overdramatic. Plenty of people had drunk sex didn't they, plenty of people didn't properly remember what had happened, did that mean we all had been assaulted? Surely not... I knew you weren't supposed to have sex while drunk full stop but I mean hadn't we all done it. It surely wasn't supposed to feel like this, I knew myself, it didn't feel like this. I had never ever felt like this.

I couldn't make eye contact with my mum or dad so my eyes settled on Samantha. My safe space. My person. The only one right now I felt I could continue being the same with. She looked back at me, her eyes knowing and she nodded. Her hair falling over her face like it always did.

'You must be Mr. Love' said Dr. Michaels reaching out her hand to my fathers and nodding hello to my mum who she had already met.

My dad stood up, followed by mum and Samantha

'Yes, can you please...explain' he looked broken, not even furious like I thought he would be, or embarrassed or something bizarre that I couldn't quite place my finger on. Something not common, a feeling I didn't know a lot about. Shame. There it was. That's what I felt. I'd never felt this before. This was a new growing inside of me. Of not being good. Of not being good enough, I shouldn't have let myself be in this situation. My father shouldn't know I had let myself get into this situation.

Dr. Michaels started to speak 'My name is Dr. Michaels and after speaking now with Scarlett I would like to refer her over to the Sexual Assault unit that we have here in the Rotunda. I believe with what has happened in Scarlett's case that the staff over there are most equipped to deal with this case, how does that sound?'

I think I zoned out, I stared out the window as I heard my mum tear up and ask did she know anymore, Samantha stayed silent, my dad sounded angry. They asked what was really happening, what did Dr. Michaels really mean. There should be a name for the language we silently speak that is hidden between the words that we actually say out loud. There should be a name for the fear this language can instill.

A lady with a cast around her arm rested her head on what might have been her husband or boyfriend as he rubbed her knee. They looked tired. A little boy cried, real snotty cry's in between loud whopping coughs as his mum who looked not a lot older than me tried to distract him with a red bear. She looked worn out and he looked scared. A lady with no hair stared blankly ahead, her face caving in it was so skinny, three women and two men all around her were talking non-stop. Their voices running over each other, no space in between. No one wanted to hear anything. The woman with no hair appeared to not notice them. These people needed help. They were sick. I wasn't sick. I wasn't sick at all. I was hurt. I was hurting. But not the kind of hurting that a cast would help, or an injection, or a bandage or hell even a morphine drip. Samantha had been on one of those when she broke her femur falling out a tree. She told me she felt nothing, right now I kind of wanted to feel that.

My kind of hurting wasn't going to be numbed away. As appealing as that sounded I wasn't sure I'd want it to be, that seemed like a tempting but dangerous option. To not feel. Feeling was all I knew. Feeling was all we had. I was sure I'd read that somewhere before 'that nothing is more beautiful than just being, feeling' But right now the feeling was just too much.

'Can we go?' I asked suddenly, looking up to my family and Dr. Michaels.

I swear I saw a flicker of relief pass over my father's face, I hate it but I think I did. It hit a part of me, his relief at this just going away for him but obviously not for me. I understood though, of course he wanted this to go away. I wanted this to go away. Surely my want for this to go away was stronger than anyone else's. Then I looked at Samantha. Her gorgeous blonde hair, biting her lips and picking the sides of nails. Two bad habits I'd spent my life trying to wear out of her, I knew they got worse if she was nervous or scared. I felt such love for her in this moment. If this had been her, if this had happened to her, what would I want for her. There were tears in her eyes. No, I couldn't let her think that this was an okay thing to happen and then to be let go of. What kind of example would that be, it wouldn't be okay for her to think that someone could do this to her and then she shouldn't do anything because I hadn't.

All my life my mum had told me 'if you don't want to do it for yourself, do it for Samantha' because she knew I would do anything for my baby sister. For my mini me. She would tell me this when I was younger and would get annoyed over things like bed time being too early, I would go to bed early if it meant Samantha would then go the bed and she needed her sleep. She would tell me this if I refused to study or do my homework, if I sat down and did it Samantha would sit me and we would end up having fun together doing it. She would tell me this when I didn't want to eat healthily, wanted to only watch tv. As I got older this turned into things like not getting angry at friends for letting me down, for trying to show others only kindness, to include everyone. To visit my family. To give to the less fortunate. At the time it had seemed like my mum was looking out for Samantha, that she was going through me to get to her, not that I minded because my love for her was bigger than all I knew. But now I realized that all along, my mum had been helping me. Had been helping me become my best self.

I thought of those words my mum had said now, if I didn't want to do this for myself right now, I could most definitely do it for Samantha. For all the Samantha's out there. The younger versions of us. The ones who needed to be shown what to do. I needed to be shown what to do but I didn't have an older sister.

I wasn't being a hassle, I needed to remind myself I hadn't done anything. I wasn't the hassle. I was simply the woman. I felt so tired, I felt so drained already. I was so scared but I was also so angry. Angry because I hadn't chosen this. Angry because I felt like he had assumed I would have wanted what happened. Angry because he felt he had a right to just take from me, use me. Why do men think they have a right up until the moment we don't oblige. We wouldn't assume we have the right to enter a strangers house unless invited in. But a man can enter a woman unless she physically fights no?

I snapped back to the waiting room. Where I had just asked if we could go. I shouldn't go. I'd never been one to go with my gut much, I generally either followed the rulebook or went completely off it on the rare occasion. But right now I had this overwhelming gut feeling that I should and most importantly that I could do this. Dr. Michaels was looking at me, she spoke.

'Scarlett if you go over to the specialised unit they will give you a few options. It is completely your choice but I really would recommend that you at least give it a go, even if it's just to put your mind at ease about potential STD's or - '

I cut her off 'no no, I'll go, let's go where is it? 'I stood up taller. I had to be stronger than I felt. I realized that I had to actually be a completely different human than the human being that I felt like right now.

Dr. Michaels looked confused but nodded with a small smile 'You can do this Scarlett, I promise you're in safe hands"

November 1st: Chris (Sexual Assault Treatment Unit Nurse)

'I wanted to connect, I wanted these patients to feel like they could

reach out their hands, their fears and for us to be there, ready to grab on tight until they felt safe again'

I love my job. I love how awful yet beautiful it is. You're probably wondering what I mean by beautiful. I mean, I am literally working in a unit that takes care of people who have been sexually assaulted. Often brutally, often under the influence, often by someone they know so extremely well. It doesn't sound like there is anything beautiful about that. There isn't. There is absolutely no beauty in someone taking advantage of another person's vulnerability, whether that vulnerability is the fact that they are a woman, that they are physically weaker, that they are drunk or young or ill or not fully able to make the choice for themselves. There is no beauty in using power to abuse, to damage, to inflict pain.

That being said, every single day when I come into work, I see so much beauty. I see it in the other nurses, who are the people that inspired me to be here in the first place. Who work every day. And smile. Every day. All day. But there is also so much beauty in their gentle touches, in their soft words, the way they offer ears and words when they have been on their feet for thirteen hours. And are more than likely going home to families that will also need their open ears and kind words. I see beauty in the brave women and men who walk through our front doors. Those terrifying front door. Who are trying, who are suddenly lost in a world they once knew. Who are lost but hope to find a safe place here. I find beauty in the fact that in a way there is a safe space in the world here for them. That this is that space. There's beauty in the hands they hold as they walk in, in the families and friends who supply endless mugs of tea because it's love in a liquid form. It's comfort, it's the best they can do right now. There's beauty in the very concept that even though it is people who have hurt those who end up here, it is still people that they turn to, to then help them. There is beauty in the fact that people simply need other people.

When I was a student nurse I did a rotation in a maternity hospital, and I was baffled by many things but the one thing I saw that stuck out with me the most was this; when you reached out to all the tiny babies hands, or even if you put your hands anywhere near their hands, they would grab on to your finger with their miniature hands and they would hang on for dear life. Their tiny fingers would curl around your one pinkie finger. Which was suddenly massive in comparison. The midwives told me it was a reflex. And an important sign that they were doing well. A reflex. Isn't that so gorgeous, that our most natural human instinct mere minutes after we are brought into this world is to hold on to another human. To connect. To feel connected. To hold tight until we feel better. That is when I knew, for me, that being a nurse wasn't going to just be my job. It was going to be my way of life. I wanted to connect, I wanted these patients to feel like they could reach out their hands, their fears and for us to be there ready to grab on tight until they felt safe again.

It was Scarlett's sister that I remembered seeing first. She walked in ahead of Scarlett, I obviously at the time didn't know her name was Scarlett, she walked in just like so many other young women. Except for the one thing I did notice, she had three people around her. That was unusual, also the three people around her looked like together they would make up a very normal conventional family. Mother and father and two daughters, I didn't at the time know who they were to each other but this is what one would presume. And this is most definitely not something we often see with sexual assault cases. It was more often than not a friend, sometimes a sibling. If the victim is young often a family member but for teenage girls in particular it was generally their best friend, again I saw the brutality but nonetheless the beauty of that. Having a family all together coming in to report, well it was the first time I saw it. It was different, a lot of the time people spoke about keeping the fact that they'd been assaulted from their family.

'Hello' said the younger looking of the two girls. Samantha, I would later find out.

'Hello, how can I help you all today' I smiled at them.

'Hi, ehm we were over in the main hospital and they told me that I needed to come here instead…sorry not needed, my doctor, she recommended' said the taller young woman.

I nodded, 'What's your name?' I asked

'Scarlett' she replied 'Scarlett Love'

'Okay Scarlett Love, what a gorgeous name, well my name is Chris. If you're family want to take a seat over there I can run you through a little bit about what happens here?'

'I can stay with her' said who I presumed was the mother. Scarlett looked uncomfortable.

'What age are you Scarlett?' I asked softly

'17' she replied 'I'm fine mum, honestly ill just see what they have to do and let you know' she looked to me as she spoke the words to her mother as if she was asking me was this the right thing to say. I nodded.

'We won't be too long, Scarlett can then have a think about what she wants to do. There tea and biscuits just around the corner' I smiled and guided Scarlett towards a small room. I had done this hundreds of times before yet these women never blended into one for me. Scarlett wasn't another woman who had been assaulted that was simply coming through the door, she was a person. I didn't know her but I did know that no one ever deserved this.

'You can have a seat Scarlet' I smiled and encouraged her to sit down. I sat down opposite her, not directly, at a 5 o'clock position. I thought back to when I had learned this model, the SOLER model in nursing. It was used to encourage open communication and make clients feel at ease. It had somehow trickled into my whole life and I found myself always having an open posture, never crossing my legs, leaning slightly towards whomever I was talking to. I did this now and Scarlet looked down at her slightly chipped nails.

'Scarlett, I am going to give you some information is that okay?'

Scarlett nodded 'there's a lot, isn't there, a lot of information. I don't even really remember what the doctor said to me....'

I smiled softly 'I know it is a lot, how about we don't think of it as information for now but just you're current options okay?'

'Okay yes, ehm before you say anything I think I do want to report this to the guards. I don't know if that is important right now but I....yeah that's what I want to do'

My stomach fluttered, so many women come in here every single day, got psychological help, get checked and tested but never reported. I don't blame them in any way, the system is not built to support them and most of them have seen or heard of someone going through the process and know how traumatic it can be. But every-time a woman says they wish to report my heart does skip a beat, with joy, with fear, more than likely with hope. Maybe this will be the one you know. Maybe this will be the case that breaks our silence and finally gives these women and men the justice they deserve. Because somewhere in our history the storyline got warped, a plot got thrown in that suggests that women 'cry rape' whenever they want. It's simply not true, out of the thousands of women that are assaulted every year, in Ireland the last figures showed that less than 32% of them reported the crime to the guards. Scarlett is in the minority.

She is one of the three people in every ten that will report. Seven out of every ten women I see go home and try to forget that this ever happened to them. Seven. Let's imagine if ten people were staying in a hotel. One night someone breaks into the hotel and robs these ten people. The next morning they are all asked if they want to tell the guards, and only three decide to report the fact that they had been robbed whilst staying in a hotel? Seven are happy to just walk away with their possession taken and expect no reimbursement or punishment for the criminal. It wouldn't happen would it? Why with sexual assault are people almost expected to not report. I'll never know. But I do know that the blame culture came about as a way of silencing victims. Never would we ever tell a person who is robbed that is their own fault for ownings things, you don't tell a child that is taken that it is their fault for being alone, you don't tell victims of a mass shooting that it is their fault for attending school. You don't tell rape victims that it is their fault for being assaulted… yet…we do?

But back to my heart skipping a beat in this little room with this young woman, 'Okay Scarlett, thank you for telling me that now because it actually is very important to this process, we would encourage everyone to report an assault but of course it is completely a person choice. But if that is what you want to do I will actually begin that process now if that's okay with you because the sooner we start the better it is for the case is that alright?'

I didn't mean to scare Scarlett, I knew I was sounding speedy but it was important. If this was what Scarlett wanted then the sooner we got started the better.

'Yes that's okay…can I report here? Or what do I do' asked Scarlett, her face was now drained of colour and it was almost as if she was working in autopilot.

'Okay, we will call the garda station that is closest to where the assault took place, they will come and take a report. Then a forensic clinical examination will be carried out by the nurses here okay? I will also be in the examination room with you while the forensic clinical examiner does the exam'

Scarlett nodded. I continued' 'We will try and make you feel as at ease as possible but you should know that it is quite an invasive examination, we will be as quick and as gentle as possible but the evidence from the examination could be really important later on okay?'

'Yeah, like a rape kit is it?' Scarlett asked.

'Exactly, we can also provide you with a support worker here would you like that?'

'A support worker?'

'Yes, the Dublin rape crisis centre offers psychological support to patients here, they are volunteers who are highly trained. It is often nice to have someone outside of the family and also someone who isn't part of the medical team too, they're just here to support you and help you through this? How does that sound to you? I asked.

'Yeah okay…sorry I'm at such a loss for words right now…this isn't me at all' Scarlett looked at me.

I nodded 'Scarlett please don't be sorry, you are doing so well. You don't have to be sorry to anyone here okay, I can only imagine how hard it is what you're experiencing right now. Were just here to support you through the process…shall we report to the guards now?'

Scarlett looked at me with such terror. But I had seen those eyes so many times. It didn't make me immune I knew that… however there was a part of me that was scared of how none of this seemed to shock me anymore. I didn't know how I felt about that. That lack of horror from terrible things and the realities I had grown to except from this world.

'Okay…will they come here?'

'As you are going to report, a guard must be here for the clinical examination. But don't worry they will stand outside the door, they won't be able to see anything. So will your support worker, it will be just two of us inside. And the clinical examiner will explain the process in more detail for you…is that all okay?'

'Yes…so I'll call the guards?' asked Scarlett.

'Yes we will assist you in calling them, find the closest station and you can explain where you are, you're situation and they will send someone over here okay?'

Scarlett nodded. 'can I go talk to my sister and then call them'

'Of course, just come up to me or the reception whenever you are ready to call them'

Scarlett took a sharp inhale, her eyes narrowing. She looked in pain.

'Where does it hurt Scarlett?' I asked gently. Her hand went to her head. 'I don't know why it's only now…I forgot…' I walked over to her, looked at back of her head. Her hair was in a bun. I touched it gently and I noted her grimace. 'It's been in that bun since, I think I might have hit it against the tiles' she said, playing with her hands.

I didn't want to hurt her. The team would be taking account of everything on her body. 'I'll tell the examination team, they will have a look just let them know whenever and wherever anything hurts okay Scarlett?'

She nodded. We both stood up and I opened the door. 'You will get to speak to your support worker before the examination too if you want?'

'I think I'll wait for after if that's okay...I think...it's just a lot of talking to a lot of people right now...is that okay?'

'Scarlett, whatever you wish is okay here. You're in a safe place and we will look after you. I'll have a support worker for you after the examination'

Scarlett smiled and walked back to her family. I contacted the Dublin Rape Crisis centre to get someone who would be Scarlett's support worker. I did my job. I went back to reception and I saw Scarlett's mum on the verge of tears, her dad motionless and her little sister talking to her. They were holding hands. The guards called with another case. Then a few minutes later, another. It was a busy day but this was our day, this was my job. This. Was. Normal.

Samantha

"we should be the ones to decide when we are sexual'

I know a lot of people who will say they look up to their big sisters. Especially if they're a lot older than them, who would say they want to be just like them. I never wanted to be just like Scarlett, I never could. We were very different people, where Scarlett saw passion I saw recklessness. Where Scarlett saw opportunity I saw fear. Where Scarlett saw mistreatment I saw the normal world. Sometimes, more often than not, I was afraid I would always live in Scarlett's shadow. And as much as I wanted to hate her for it, I couldn't. Because all Scarlett ever wanted was the world, but not for herself, for me too.

. . .

'I can't do it' I said for the third time that night, staring hopelessly at the mound of clay in front of me. The mound of clay that had not changed shape in the last three hours. Scarlett leaped over from behind the couch, where she had been scribbling away into one of her many journals.

'I'm so dumb, why can't I think of anything, anything at all..' I sighed

'I don't like those words, that's my sister you're talking about' she said sitting down next to me on the floor. Scarlett always said that if I was ever saying something bad about myself, or giving out. It made me smile.

Our mum always let me take over the 'play room' whenever I was asked to make a piece or wanted to. I had been playing with clay since a baby. In school I won lots of competitions and my pieces were being shown in little places like libraries and art cafes, but now I had been asked to create a piece for a major young adult competition. I couldn't do it.

'I can't though, I don't even know what it's supposed to be yet'

'None of us do' laughed Scarlett. I rolled my eyes. But tears were prickling behind them. Scarlett seemed to take everything in her stride, nothing phased her. Nothing was too hard. Where did she get that confidence because it certainly was genetic. I can testify to that.

'Hey, little one...' Scarlett put her arm around me. 'Come on missy, tell me what you want it to be'

'I don't know, I just...I want it to be beautiful, I want people to look at it and feel something. See something they can relate to... but how can everyone relate to one thing'

'Hmm...Sammy, to me everything you make it beautiful...but something everyone can relate to huh?'

I nodded, wiping my tears away.

'You're going to do it, and you're going to blow them all away I just know it. One of these days I'll have to go around the world to see you in different art galleries and you'll barely have time to acknowledge me at the back of the crowd eh?' Scarlett nudged me.

'Well that's never going to happen' I sighed 'if I can't even make one piece'

'That's a lie, you've made hundreds of pieces'

'Well none of them mattered, this is the important one'

'That's another lie' said Scarlett 'every single one of them mattered and don't you every forget that'

'Why?' I asked

'Because they got you here didn't they?' she smiled and kissed my cheek 'you've got this little one, you're more talented than everyone I know combined'

And I did get it. It came to me there and then. I jumped up. I ran up to my room and grabbed my folder full of all my past pieces. I ran back downstairs to Scarlett who had retreated back to the couch with her journal. I started sketching, I combined all the pieces that I had made. All the parts of me that got me here today. And in Scarlett's words 'I made something beautiful out of all the parts of me'

I love my sister. When my sister stood in our kitchen that first morning in November I had never felt so cold. So cold because the warmth was no longer there. Scarlett was my warmth. She was our fire. You couldn't put into words exactly what Scarlett was like, a lot of my friends were obsessed with her, thought she was so gorgeous, so together, so collected and cool. Other friends of mine thought she was too much, too out there, too vocal. I knew that most of the people in Scarlett's year didn't actually think too much about her, she was fairly quiet in school and wouldn't have been the most social person. She had her group and she loved them and that was that for Scarlett. People rarely paid her attention and she liked that. As much as Scarlett could handle the spotlight well, she hated it. When our granny died she had asked that Scarlett speak at the funeral, probably because my granny and Scarlett had a bond that no one really understood. I mean I loved my granny but her and Scarlett were like twin sisters or something. But I think she also asked her because she knew it would really push Scarlett's comfort zone and Nanny Lola had always loved to push her children and grandkids where she could. My mum often complained of how controlling she was, we would laugh and tell her she meant well but sigh as we now realized we had to call various aunts and uncles on behalf of Nanny Lola just to say hi.

I'm getting very off track, but I guess it's nice to think and to talk about the things that don't revolve around Scarlett's assault because that is only one singular event in the massive plotline that is Scarlett's life, that is all our life's. I think that's been forgotten. That we are more than just a case. My friends and my boyfriend are all now constantly asking me about Scarlett, how she is, how did this happen, what did she do. And I feel like screaming. Because it's as if they see a different Scarlett now. I suddenly don't just have a big sister. I am now the little sister of the girl who said she was raped. There's always the 'said' included in the sentences also. Never the little sister of the girl who 'was' raped.

Back when I was sitting in that waiting room with mum and dad. They had been holding hands and I didn't know what to do with mine, I wished I had clay in them. Something to keep them busy. I realized in that moment how important it could be to have another person to make things softer in life. Right now it would have been me and Scarlett holding hands, we were the other duo in our family. The other pair.

Scarlett was in getting an examination. A rape kit. That was something I thought I would only have to hear about in crime documentaries. But no, here I was while my big sister got one. I didn't know what to say to my parents. I didn't know what would be right or normal for me to do. What if they got angry at me for saying the wrong thing.

My mum turned to me, 'Scarlett will need something to eat after all this' she said. Dad didn't even move slightly as she spoke. 'Okay' I nodded, glad of something normal being said. 'I'll go to the café and get her something, do you want anything?' I stood up, picking my jacket off the back of the chair. My mum looked to my dad, he was there but he wasn't. 'Not now honey thank you' I nodded and walked towards the exit. When I got out into the cold air I stopped. I looked up and then I looked behind. I wished I could just never walk back through those two doors again. I wished that I had absolutely no idea what the inside of that building looked like. But I did. I put on my jacket as the wind howled around me and I started walking towards the main part of James's hospital. As I was walking I started to think about what Scarlett had been wearing. I knew it should be irrelevant but I also knew the judgement most women get for wearing or being too much or too little. I had seen Maddy's stories on Instagram the night before and her and Scarlett were an angel and a devil. Scarlett of course being the devil naturally. That would have normally made me laugh but right now it made me shiver. I found the main entrance and followed the signs towards a coffee shop. I got into the queue and I noticed the people around me. Many of them were patients, backs exposed through their hospital gown. These people had their bare skin on display yet they weren't being sexualised the way I knew Scarlett and myself and every girl I knew would be when our backs or thighs, or anything were displayed. I stared at these people and I thought, not wearing clothes doesn't automatically give someone a right to sexualise a person. We should be the ones to decide when we are sexual. When we want to be sexual. Seeing these patients made me think of how often a person is naked and not sexual. Here they were semi naked and not at all sexual, most of them were probably getting surgeries that might require them to be fully naked. We are literally naked when we are born, when we shower, sometimes we can be naked when we swim or sleep. We are very often naked in art. In none of these occasions are we being sexual yet we are being naked. Being naked cannot be used as a tool against us. Showing too much skin cannot be a weapon against a woman.

'Excuse me, excuse me' I snapped back to reality. I was holding up the queue. A bright eyed young girl was on the other side of the counter smiling back at me 'You alright honey?' she asked kindly. 'Oh ehm yes sorry can I get a hot chocolate please, oh actually two and ehm' I scanned the clear glass cabinet 'two of those' I pointed at two ready- made wraps. I was very literally buying food for the sake of something to do but for me right now that was reason enough.

When I look back on that day, it all feels like a blur and I don't really remember it well but I do remember the feelings. I remember feeling helpless. I remember feeling as though I had never wished so strongly to absolutely change the past. I had, like most people, had my moments that I wished I could go back and do a little differently but never anything like this. I'd always thought it was happening for a reason, that it would bring me where I wanted, I didn't think that this served a purpose. And if it did, I didn't know if understood this world anymore.

Suki (Rape Crisis Centre support worker)

*'There was a gap where our words used to fill,
a silence where laughter once lived'*

The one thing that I've never been able to shake about sexual assault, even before I knew anything much about it, back when rapist was just a word whispered in the school yard about the slightly odd looking men in the town. Terrible I know. We didn't really know what it meant, but even before I understood the full extent and range of what sexual assault is and can be and is becoming. Even as a young teenager when I knew the bare minimum, what always bothered me was that no matter what, the victim could never just be purely innocent. The way that other victims in different crimes were. There is no other crime where victim blaming is as prevalent as it is in sexual assault. Because even if you won your case, even if your assaulter is locked up for life. Even when you clearly innocent, you are still guilty. People will find you guilty of something, you're guilty of being too drunk, however if the perpetrator is drunk when he assaults you it translates to 'he was too drunk he didn't know what he was doing' but if it's the victim that is too drunk it somehow becomes 'how could she let herself get into that state, who's to blame really'. You're guilty of being under-dressed, of being too tempting, too pretty, or in some cases not pretty enough. It is no joke that far too many articles have been released about how the perpetrator was too attractive to 'need' to rape someone. That the victim wasn't even 'that' pretty, or that the victim wasn't pretty 'enough' to be raped so why would they even bother. But on the flip side of that, there's the too pretty, the tempting victims. Whom the perpetrators clearly couldn't resist. They shouldn't look so nice, they shouldn't dress like that. That skirts too short, her tops too low, her boobs are too big, stockings. Seriously...how could she not have expected this. You know boys. They can't help themselves.

This lack of taking responsibility for ones actions has always drove me crazy. Not that I show this of course, I've been a woman long enough to know that if I show how mad so many things get me, then I won't win any of the battles. It's a delicate balance. It's a pick or mix. We have to decide what we care about the most and we have to put our full fight into that. Even if homelessness bothers me, so does female genital mutilation in third world countries, oh and the fact that domestic violence is the number one killer of women worldwide, also that we live in a world where boys are being raised on porn and girls are being raised on Disney movies where a prince saves them, as well as the fact that some people think it's still funny to call something gay, and don't even get me started on the fact that women's sex lives are still nowhere near as fulfilling as men's. But we can't spend our days angry at the world. I'm not saying that we can't fight for all of these things because I fully believe that all of them and many more are worth fighting for. I suppose that I have just realized that for myself I can't do it.

When I was around 18 I got angry. I got angry at the world, for all of these misjustices and the rest. I went to every march and protest and strike and revolt. I waved banners and flags and shouted and marched and sang and danced and stripped in slut walks, I ran for the underprivileged, I raised money for the addicts. I refused to eat this or that. I wouldn't be told what to do. I felt so much. But as time went on I realized my passion was becoming misplaced. I had so much fight in me that I had forgotten who I was really fighting for. I was suddenly just fighting the world. I had forgotten the people at the heart of the mistreatment. The real reason we were all putting our time and energy into these activities wasn't because we all got a kick out of screaming down the streets or we really loved knocking on door after door or honestly it just was our idea of a great afternoon to stand in the street and ask people to sign a piece of paper that would more than likely be dismissed. No, we did this because we cared deeply about other humans, and about how they were treated. I had forgotten that I did love this world and that was why I wanted it so badly to be a better place. But really I had forgotten me. I had spent my young adult years, the end of secondary school but mostly college, being angry and I didn't want to be like that anymore. I wanted to see the good in the world again, fully knowing that it lived closely alongside the bad. But I wanted my glass to be half full instead of half empty again. And focusing on the bad, as much as I admired the people who relentlessly fought for what the world needed, I personally just couldn't do it anymore.

Once I left college with my degree in politics and sociology I finally told myself the truth. I had been hurting and this had been my way of healing.

When I was 17 I was at one of my friend's houses. The group of us there had known each other since we were sipping juice boxes on the playground floor. Now we were sipping corona's and playing beer pong. These people were my family, we'd done it all together up until know. Parties and first loves, break-ups and road-trips, getting our driver's license, being given our own key to our homes. Passing exams, failing them, we know our lives would probably all head in different directions soon. But we had our plans for the yearly reunions, the overlap in trips abroad. We helped each other decide what we wanted to do with our lives once this fairy-tale teenage dream we were living in ended. We were a team, we supported and accepted all of each other's quirks and whims.

Until one moment, one moment where I woke up and was underneath one of these people. These boys and girls I called my family.

This boy I had trusted. This boy that I would have called if I had been upset or stuck or happy or annoyed.

I had taken one too many sips, I had fallen asleep and now here I was. I had believed I was in a safe place. Up until this moment I didn't even know there was such a thing as bad places. But now I was confused. When I heard about people being raped, I always heard about how brutal it was. Or how a woman was lost after a party, by herself in the night club, walking home alone. Was lured somewhere, was tricked, was taken, was hurt. Strangers equalled danger. Danger. Danger. Danger. Stranger danger. This wasn't danger, this was my friends. The people I loved and trusted the most must have been mere meters away. I wasn't lured anywhere, I wasn't alone, I had wanted to be here but I hadn't wanted this.

I was even more confused because I had kissed him. I remembered that. And I remembered that I didn't want to do much more but I also knew that kissing someone didn't translate to I will sleep with you after. That's what I knew. That's what I thought I knew. However somewhere in that kiss, I took it as just a kiss and he took it as permission to let me lay back, drifting in and out, and have sex with me.

What's even more confusing was that as soon as I realized what was really happening it was almost over. And the minute it ended I felt like the guilty one. I hadn't said no. I had kissed him and I hadn't pushed him off me when I realized what was happening.

I stumbled away, away from him. Confused and blurry. Back to be bed with all my other so called family. I fell asleep in a house that up until that moment I would have called a home. In that moment I didn't really think anything was wrong. But my head was sore and fuzzy and I think my shock meant that I couldn't fully comprehend what had just happened.

We parted ways. I pushed it down but it wasn't long before I realized I didn't see any of my so called family anymore.

I don't really know if what happened was wrong. I don't actually know how much permission I gave him or how little I was conscious enough to do so.

I know that I tell people on a daily basis now that if someone is drunk or sick it means they are not actually able to give consent so I therefore technically did not give it. But did he know that? I know if I heard my own story told to me from someone else I would think that they had been taken advantage of but it's not as easy to tell that to yourself. No one wants to be a victim. Because as I said in the beginning, in these cases the victim is never not seen as somewhat guilty. I could see myself guilty of so many things, I was guilty of being too drunk, I was guilty of probably being a flirt, I was guilty of letting him kiss me. I was guilty of kissing many of the boys I knew. I was guilty of often being a girl amongst groups of boys. None of these are crimes, in any other context these are the very normal activities of almost everyone. Drinking and kissing is normal.

But in a court room, in front of twelve faces, these are what will be focused on. Exactly how much had I had to drink? Do I usually drink that much? Why did I kiss him if I didn't want anything else? Did I kiss a lot of my friends? If I was conscious enough to kiss him surely I was conscious enough to not have sex with him? If I realized it was happening why didn't I stop it? Why didn't I scream if my friends were so close by? Why didn't I say anything to him after? Why didn't I tell my friends? If these people were like my family how did they now know? How could it have been that bad if I went straight to bed?

The answers. I don't know. No answer seemed right. So I still don't know if what he did was wrong.

I don't know what it was. I don't know what to call it.

But I do know I was so scared of ever seeing him again, I was scared of going there again. At the time it wasn't too hard, we were all going our different ways. Some of us were moving away for work, some of us were going to college, some of us were travelling. Maybe the drift was inevitable. But I can't help but remember me, and remember how much I loved that friend family we had created, and I can't help but know in my gut that I would not have wanted to let that family go.

If I'm being honest it took me a while to move on, it was living with me in ways I didn't even realize for a while. In my sudden fear of certain things. I pinpointed it to the fact that I was now being more mature and aware of the dangers that were out there, that in my youth I had been naïve.

I'm 36 years old now and I still don't know if what he did was wrong. I don't think he has any idea of what he did. I did bump into him over the course of my life a few times. But I never said a word. I never wanted to. I knew how people who spoke their story out loud like this were treated and it scared me. It scared me more than living without telling. There was nothing to back me up, absolutely nothing and at the end of the day it was my word against his. That was all.

Is it messed up of me to wish that there had been more of a struggle? Is it wrong of me to wish it had been more violent so then I would know for sure that it was wrong. I wish I had shouted, I wish I had screamed, I wish I had realized what was happening and scratched his face. Or what if I had bruises or had yelled for help. Because if there had been more of a struggle wouldn't that prove that I didn't want it? If I had stained his face wouldn't that show I was fighting back? If someone had heard me screaming wouldn't that mean that I had in fact asked for help. Instead I had not even realized, I had lain there. Instead my mouth was zipped shut by me and me alone. Instead my body didn't move until it was over. I wish I had been tear streaked and sobbing as I ran back into the house because then wouldn't someone have noticed and seen the damage done? But no, I walked away by myself and I wiped my eyes. Is it messed up of me to wish my assault had been more violent because if it did, maybe I would have been forced to be brave enough to tell.

I have a family now, a husband I love, two boys, one girl. My husband doesn't know about that night, not really. I think at the very beginning of our relationship I may have alluded to it, the memories were fresher when we met and I thought it was important that he knew everything about me. What would I do if this snuck up from behind in the future and hit me right when I was having sex with him. What if he said something and it triggered a memory I didn't even know I had and I lashed out on him for no reason. What if he touched me in a certain way. What if, what if. So I let out a mention here or there, mostly when a little bit tipsy. The liquid giving me courage. Never giving any details, saying there had been an incident 'nothing too bad' he never pushed, he just listened. Told me I could tell him anything. I knew I could, but did I want to. I wondered about what he would think of me, would it cross his mind a lot too, would it change how he viewed our relationship, would it bring up issues I never even knew could exist. I also considered me, did I want him to know, would I only then spend my time thinking about how maybe he pitied me, or didn't fully believe me, or felt hesitant now. I know a lot of people might think you should really be able to tell your husband, if he loves you it won't make a difference. But I was technically able to tell him and I knew he loved me enough but no one could ever promise me that it wouldn't make a difference. No one could guarantee me that it wouldn't turn my world upside down. I had told only a few people but enough people to know it did.

I never told anyone during school. It wasn't until I went to college. They didn't know him. It felt different, they wouldn't have any preconceived ideas about him. All he would be to them was the guy who assaulted their friend. This was important to me. I don't know why but a part of me still didn't want to ruin his life, I mean I wanted to, I really wanted him to pay for the pain he had brought me, the way he had changed my life in the worst of ways. But I knew ruining his life for what he had done to me involved another part of me getting ruined in the process.

One of my friends felt so sorry for me we actually couldn't remain friends. Another friend of mine told me I was probably just drunk and being a bit dramatic. Another friend listened, teared up, told me I was amazing, hugged me, but things were never ever the same between us. There was a gap where our words used to fill, a silence where laughter once lived.

Of course, there are my best friends. Who are still my best friends today. These people, they know everything. When I have the freak outs and the fear, they teach my bravery. They hold my hand until I don't need them to anymore and the let me go just when I'm the step below ready because we both now that ready will never come. They can put him in a sentence and end that sentence with a joke, without it feeling like they're not taking me seriously. They can add a note of lightness to the subject. They can make me feel like me. Not like a defect of the person I once was. Not like a crime scene.

I'm sure this is the case for many people in my situation. This something that happened to me when I was young. There's millions of versions of them out there, all with the one underlying thing in common 'I don't know what it was but it didn't feel right'

. . .

But this was how I ended up where I was today. November 1st, sitting in the in between waiting room waiting for a young girl I hadn't met yet called Scarlett to be finished her examination. As I waited with my coffee in hand I thought about all the years I had been doing this now. I was starting to question if this was the right thing for me to be doing. To be dedicating so much of my life to the noisy horrible part of the world. To spend my life helping people who had been through what I knew was my biggest challenge. It meant I never forgot it. My volunteering revolved around it, I also worked as a social worker so my work there revolved a lot around it too. Was this healing? Was constantly thinking about and being reminded about the only thing in my life I wanted to forget the best way to move forward? Yet I found magic in empathy, I knowing there was others and that maybe perhaps my simple presence could help. Could fill that gap that I was never brave enough to explore myself. Maybe this was my bravery. Or maybe I was sitting here every week waiting to see what these girls had that I could never muster up. Searching them for a courage I could never obtain.

Scarlett walked out. She was pale and beautiful and had the look behind her eyes that I found so many young girls here had. The look of dissociation, of 'am I really doing this, is this really happening'

'Hi Scarlet' I stood up and introduced myself to her. 'I'm Suki, I'm your support worker from the Dublin Rape Crisis Centre, I can help you with any question or really anything that comes up for you'

'Hi Suki, thanks...thank you for doing this stuff...should we go back to my family or can I stay here for a minute?'

'We can stay here for a minute' I smiled and sat back down, patting to the seat next to me. I handed Scarlett a hot chocolate I had gotten her. 'Sorry it's hot chocolate but it's probably more along the lines of warm chocolate now' Scarlett attempted a smile.

'So what do people usually need a support worker for?' she asked me, looking me straight in the eye. This girl had a presence to her. You got a sense of something just being around her. I hoped for her that this process didn't take it away.

'Well' I started, taking a sip 'we're mainly here as a sort of uninvolved resource. I'm not a family member or a friend so it's a bit easier for me to be objectively supportive and help you with any of the practical question'

Scarlett nodded. 'I've heard about support workers, we got a talk from the Rape Crisis place in TY…I always wondered how good a person would have to be to give up their time to do what you do..for free…I think I was young though. I can easily see how someone would do it now….'

I nodded. Scarlett looked at me. 'Why do you do this?'

I looked straight back at her, I had never been asked this. Which was surprising when I think of it now. I always admired people who volunteered, I still do but I have realized that I feel better about myself for doing it so I don't know what that says about me. I feel less unwired if I am concentrating on helping someone else.

'I do this…I guess I do this because I really think you're all incredible women, and I think this is an incredible service and I guess it's just me doing my bit…' I took a sip of my drink. Scarlett looked at me funnily, 'what, you think we are incredible women because we've just been assaulted?" she said bluntly and directly. I regretted my words immediately, of course I didn't think they were incredible because of that, I thought they were incredible because of how they moved forward with it. But words weren't going to do that justice. So I did what I was taught in my training and I neutralized the situation.

'I'm sorry Scarlett, that was not a correct choice of words. Is there anything you've got any questions about right now?' I asked as she sat down next to me.

'Sorry, I snapped there...' said Scarlett.

'Please don't apologize, it's a very intense time for you at the moment'

'The forensic examiner... he said I had some sort of head trauma, there was blood and stuff...he had to put in two stitches' she touched the back of her head gingerly.

'Okay, they'll bring those kits to a centre in phoenix park now and everything will be tested there' I said, information was key is what we were taught to pass on to our clients. If someone is more aware of what is going on, they feel more in control of the situation.

'I'm scared' Scarlett said softly, her hands wrapped around the hot chocolate. I nodded slowly…..Scarlett mumbled something so softly I couldn't make it out.

'Sorry Scarlett?' I asked and she continued to look down at her drink.

'I know him so well, David I mean, I just don't know why he would do this' she looked at me. As far as I'd been told Scarlett hadn't yet disclosed who the perpetrator was so I wanted to hold this information carefully.

'I tried to get him off me, he knew it was wrong. I know he knew, her hurt me' Scarlett's voice cracked 'I would have trusted him, I don't….I don't know why I am doing this…'

'Doing this?' I asked

'This, this whole exam, I told that nurse that I wanted to tell the guards, they're here already....but it's different...David's not a stranger....I've been with him before. I'm not stupid I know how these things go Suki...I know how I look right now' she was crying now. I thought of how overwhelmed she must feel, I genuinely myself could not even imagine how I would be behaving in this situation.

'I know it's difficult to think about the circumstances around what has happened, but the most important thing is that you know what he did was wrong Scarlett'

'I was drunk. I was looking for Joel...and then I was in the bathroom and David...he was hurting me...he was inside me and I froze Suki...I was so scared and it hurt so much. He's so much bigger than me...the tiles were so cold'

My heart broke, yet I'd heard it all before. Different names, different places but someone you trust and somewhere you're safe.

'I know I blacked out...but that was only in the bathroom with him, when I hit my head...then when I woke up he was having sex with me...I think I scratched him..'

'You scratched him?' I asked, trying to remain neutral but also thinking it would be the slightest piece of evidence for her case.

'Yes...then he was gone...once he had enough I think.....they've given me the morning after pill....and have taken my blood.... I don't know...you know when your body goes into autopilot?'

I nodded

'I think that's what happened...I walked straight to Liv's room... I couldn't even think really..'

'Our body's responses to trauma are not always what we expect' I said softly.

'Yeah' Scarlett's body language changed, I'd seen it many times before. Her talking was over I guessed. Her body was going to close up.

'I should go back to my family...I have to talk to the guards too...' she stood up.

'Thank you Suki...'

'Not at all Scarlett...I'll be here until you're ready to leave so if you want to chat again or have any question please come to me' I smiled and stood up with her.

She nodded and I walked after her as she went back to her family. Her little sister took her hand immediately. I gave them all a small smile and I headed into the office. To hand over anything. I might never speak to Scarlett again, I may never know what happens to her or her family. But the next time I was on call in a week or two, I will get a phone call call, I will get a case and I'd head back here to the SATU and I'd sit outside the room and wait for another woman. And I and so many others would continue to do this until the world learns.

3

In another version of this life.

Scarlett

'All of those choices will now seem somehow much more important than his choice and my lack thereof'

Some people believe that we have parallel lives. Some people truly believe that there are hundreds, thousands, maybe even millions of different versions of us out there, depending on the amount of seemingly insignificant choices we make each and every day. That sometimes a simple yes or no. Or staying in instead of going out can change the course of our life forever. Or imagine you hadn't kissed that one boy on that one night, how much of an impact could that have made? Imagine you hadn't gone to that school or what if you had been sick on a certain day.

They believe that this one life can't be it, that we have to be experiencing all of the alternative choices we could make. That we can easily shift into another version of our lives. That they co-exist with us but we can't see them. Some people believe in this.

I don't know how much I believe in parallel lives. But I often think of one.

I think of if I hadn't walked down the stairs to my family the next morning, what if I had just taken some Panadol and fallen asleep. Not to die, no, but just to sleep through the first few painful hours. Maybe if I had woken up a few hours later, when dinner was ready, maybe I would have felt more rested. Maybe I would have apologized to mum for not responding the night before, for getting drunk. And maybe then I would have watched movies with Samantha all evening. I would have probably made my infamous Toblerone cheesecake as means of apology and the hungover Scarlett would turn into a family joke laughed about at Christmas time.

Or maybe my life took a different turn much earlier. Maybe I shouldn't have gone into the bathroom alone after seeing that Joel was at the party, then I wouldn't have seen the bottle of wine and if I just hadn't been so drunk.... or maybe it's that I should never have approached Joel at all.

What if just seeing him had upset me so much that instead of talking to him I cried to Bee and Liv and Maddy and I went to bed early. What if I had dressed as something else.

But perhaps it's way later, it could be in the car. What if I had stopped my mum from texting my dad. What if when I got to the hospital I told Dr. Michaels that it was all a mistake and I wanted to go home. Maybe it would never have been spoken about again. I could have simply not walked behind the hospital to the SATU centre, my family would have done whatever I said. We could have all got in the car and returned to our normal lives. Maybe I should have left half way through the statement. Or what if I hadn't felt the pain in my head and then there was no real evidence of violence and my case would have been shut down from the start. Would that have saved me something? Or would that have made things much worse.

I don't know where my parallel life started. And I don't know where she is now. I don't feel close to her in the way people believe our parallel lives to run. She feels a million miles away.

I don't know where along the way that there was a single second that occurred in which my life was irreversibly changed. If I'm to be brutally honest. My life was irreversibly changed the minute he started assaulting me. And that is a choice I did not make. That is the one action in all of this that was completely out of my control.

There is me, making my life choices. Picking my school, getting up in the morning, going to class. Going out with my friends, drinking with my friends, having coffee with them, dancing with them on the dancefloor, in our bedrooms, anywhere we can. There is me making dinner with my mom, there is me and her bringing the next door neighbours kids to the park every weekend since their mum got sick. There is me and my dad driving to piano lessons, singing along to Bruce Springsteen. There is me running, by myself with my music blaring through headphones. There is me watching movies with my sister. There is me fighting with my sister, hugging my sister, telling my sister everything will always be okay. There is me falling asleep in English but wide awake in maths, there is me thinking of how lucky I am. There is me falling in love. There is me having my heart heartbroken. There is me having sex. There is me speaking at my granny's funeral from her favourite book of poetry. There is me wearing a devils outfit for Halloween. There is me getting an award for public speaking when I was 12. There is me reading. There is me showering. There is me singing in the shower. There is me climbing trees as a child, and still climbing the same tree years later. There is me posting pictures. There is me taking photos. There is me writing memories. There is me laughing. There is me crying. There is me scrapbooking. There is me having no idea what I am feeling because I am so young but there is me knowing that a good laugh with my friends can cure nearly everything right now. There is me catching planes, and trains. There is me excited to travel the world. There is me. There is me. There is me.

All of the choices I have made in my life, up to this date, because of the one choice I did not make will now be examined.

Most especially what I wore, what I drank, who I hung out with, who I slept with. All of those choices will now seem somehow much more important than his choice and my lack thereof. Because I chose to have sex with other people it appears I therefore do not have a choice when someone decides to have sex with me. Because I chose to wear a short skirt one day means I do not have a choice if someone wolf whistles at me or tries to grab me under it. Because I chose to take a drink means I do not have a choice if someone choses to take advantage of the fact that I am drunk.

I think about the life where I am not examined. Where I am not picked apart like a science experiment. Where I am treated like a normal human being. A flawed, imperfect human being. I don't know how it came to be that a woman needed to be perfect in order to not deserve getting assaulted. I don't know how it came to be that her character and who she was or how she behaved actually mattered. I don't know who we think we are to judge someone else and decide that they were more likely to end up being assaulted.

However I would be lying if I said I didn't think about this other life, the life of not telling, of not making any statements, of not standing in court and avoiding eye contact and being constantly on edge and I really do wonder.

Would it have haunted me forever? Would it have been worse to not tell.

Because I know that's what most women do. We think about our own circumstances, our own experience of sexual assault and we think - well maybe it wasn't quite 'bad' enough to report. It wasn't clear enough or violent enough. It is always 'bad' enough to report. But I can't say for certain that reporting was this magic brave move that made my life better. In fact, for a little while it made my life subjectively much worse. But that being said I have no other version of my life to compare it to.

I often envy the version of me out there that didn't tell, which I know is an imaginary thing to envy. But I do. I miss something I never even had. Someone that doesn't even exist. But maybe if I hadn't told I would feel the exact same way. I would also long for the alternative. Maybe I would think that telling would heal me, in a way it has but it has also brought about new wounds. But again I don't know the other wounds that not telling would have brought about. I think of the quote that talks about how we can never make a fully informed decision because we have no past lives to compare to and no future life to perfect our decisions in. We have no idea. And even if we have those parallel lives, they still don't affect the way it feels in our way of life.

But I will say this.

If I could go back to the very start of the versions of me out there. The beginning of my life, before my life have even really begun and if I could make it completely different and be born a boy. I still wouldn't.

If I had been born a boy I would have no idea of the fears of the women around me. Not fully.

I wouldn't know what it felt like to have your location sent to your best friends anytime you go on a first date, or a second or third.

I wouldn't know that before even getting into a taxi alone you may have already sent the number plate and you live location to your friend, that you will sit behind the driver because that is the safest place should they try and attack you.

I wouldn't know what it felt like to always go to the bathroom in two's, sure half because it's great to chat but also half because you really don't want to be that girl in the club alone.

I wouldn't know what it's like to not put your earphones in when walking or running in the dark because if you put them in you won't hear someone coming up from behind you.

I wouldn't know the shame you feel after boys grab your bum on a night out.

I wouldn't know what it feels like to be called a slut and frigid in the same night. Sometimes the same sentence

What it's like to not know how to respond when a boy says something vulgar to you. In front of a group.

What it's like to laugh at something that isn't funny simply because all the boys are laughing and you don't want them to think your uptight and can't take a laugh and then to feel shame for giving in to their laughter afterwards.

I wouldn't know what it's like to be afraid to open the door to a man when home alone, even if that man was the mailman you've had for ten years your heart would not stop pounding until there was a safely closed door between you two.

I wouldn't know the fear in your heart when they block your way. When they side step you. When they push you to the side. Because what if this time it's not just a joke.

The sinking feeling you get when you see them crowded together looking at you as you make you way into the pubs and clubs. The groups that gather around you then once your inside these clubs and pubs.

The comments on the dance floor, of either keep going if you're doing that for me or calm down if you look like you're having too much fun without me.

I wouldn't know what it was like to walk the wrong way before the right way home when you think someone is behind you. Or to walk a different, longer way home to avoid a certain area or alley or person.

Of taxis instead of walking once its past a certain time. Of running when you can't afford a taxi but you know it isn't safe to walk.

What it's like to fake phone calls, to have lone one way conversations with yourself. To tell an imaginary someone that you'll be home soon. To make it clear that the imaginary someone is always a male. Always your boyfriend or your brother. To not be able to sleep unless you knew your friends got home safe.

To master the evasion of eye contact. To look at your feet. To know your feet so well. To sometimes walk in such a way so that your hips don't swing too much and you look smaller. To make yourself smaller. To stand out less.

I wouldn't know that attention often means harassment that we are then told is our fault because we brought about the attention in the first place. Simply by being. That this can't be their fault. That boys will be boys.

I wouldn't know the feeling of hearing those passing comments, ignoring the cat calls from cars, but aren't those humans that are inside the car.

The 'why won't you kiss me',

the 'where's your boyfriend then',

the 'well if you don't have a boyfriend…',

'why won't you do this',

'why won't you smile more',

'why won't you laugh at my jokes',

'why won't you be more easy-going?'.

Why. Why. Why.

I wouldn't know. I know there are many other different things that I would be thinking if I were a boy. I know that having these fears doesn't reflect well on either sex. I know that. I know that is not a representation of every male I know. But I also know it is a fear I cannot shake. It is a knowledge I cannot unknow.

So maybe in another turn of events I didn't tell. Maybe it slowly creeps away into the back of my mind. Only making appearances late at night when everything can feel worse anyways. Only sneaking up on me when I think I see the back of his head in a crowd. Only tightening my chest when a boy grabs a part of me in the club. Only making my heart drop when I can't find my friends. Only making me cry when I am drunk and feel as though I can't stop the tears. Only making me stomach turn when I hear of another story like mine. Only reminding me when I realize I will no longer walk there alone. I will no longer do that, go there, see them.

But maybe that would have been better than having my life broken into pieces and examined as individual actions rather than being looked at as the making up of a human being.

I do not know. I'll never know.

Because having experienced what it is like to have your life ripped to shreds by people you don't know who don't know you and are very literally getting paid to ask you excruciatingly private details about your life in front of a sea of strangers who will then misrepresent what you actually meant in a paper or a magazine or the tv. Who will then twist your words until you can't even believe you said it, who will describe you in such a way that you will think twice about how you look every time you pass a mirror. Having experienced that I can't say that the process was healing. In the end, for me, the process helped me, helped others after me but it also hurt me.

It is a price I didn't know I would pay. My courage resulted in more scars. My bravery equalled many more hours thinking and talking about my assault. Me opening my mouth and speaking those words meant I would now spend years hearing the twisted responses to my truth.

In my other life what it the price to pay. Does healing begin right away.

I don't know. I'll never know. We shouldn't have to question which choice we should make in these situations. It should be an automatic assumption that getting justice for a crime would be the best way forward. But in cases like mine there is no winning or losing. There is no right or wrong way to heal or deal or cope or move on. This is the life I have, this is all I know. Telling was the choice that I made. Most of me is glad of this…..but if there is a parallel version of me out there, I wonder how she is.

4

Before the Trial

Sam (Garda)

"So vicious and uncaring and violent, but the truth is we wouldn't know a perpetrator if we saw them"

*A*nyone who glanced at Joel Andrews would automatically think, vain, flirty young man. From his expensive shoes and old school band t-shirt, you knew he cared immensely about where he shopped but also wanted to look like minimal effort went into his attire. The sort of look that says I might judge you if the majority of your clothes aren't vintage or pre-owned. Okay maybe not everyone would think like this but I was a garda officer, a policeman. Our eyes had been trained differently. I remember on one of my first days in McCann Barracks, which is where we were all trained. A small group of us were with one of the senior trainers and he turned to us and said 'listen lads. It's like a magic show, they will try and show you something over here on the left so that you don't see what's actually happening over here on the right'

I don't know where he got this line from. But I've never stopped applying it to all aspects of my life, even outside of my career.

Joel was the kind of boy I just knew my fifteen-year-old girls would find 'good-looking'. Even though he was four years older than them. I'm not sure how I felt about their idolising of these male figures, but I suppose when I was young I had posters of half-naked women on motorbikes in my room. At least the posters they had up were a lot more PG. Thinking about it now I can't believe it was actually normal for me to have those posters in my room.

Walking into my interview room right now Joel actually resembled the exact band member that they had taped up on their bedroom wall. I told him to take a seat. He nodded, his too long hair falling over his eyes. His fingers tapping away at his upper knee. My co-worked Alex was sitting next to me. He introduced himself and myself to Joel and explained a bit about what was going on.

'Joel, can you tell me about your movements on the night of October 31st' I asked, diving straight in.

Joel sighed, and brushed his long hair out of eyes. He looked uncomfortable.

'I don't really know why I'm here, I know it has to do with Scarlett. I did see her there, I was with her…I've been hearing things…Is she okay?'

'Just walk me through your night please'

He shrugged 'shouldn't I have someone here with me?'

'Well you are nineteen years old, if you want a representative you are entitled to one but as of right now no charges are being made against you we are just trying to piece together a potential crime'

'A potential crime?' Joel asked.

I nodded. 'So you were at a party?"

I really didn't like these types of cases. They made me uncomfortable. I had told my wife this a few years ago while working on a pretty nasty sexual assault case. Three young girls, one man. The assaults had been going on for years. 'Murder, fine, battery, assault, all fine. But Maria when it's a sexual assault I just the this….this anxious feeling in my stomach….' I told her as we were getting ready for bed one night. Maria was a lecturer in UCD. Sciences.

'Why do you think that is?' she asked, hopping into the bed next to me. I turned to face her. 'I don't know, I don't like them. Nothing ever goes right, I don't….I just I get this horrible feeling like I want to leave every interview room and crime scene that's related to them…even if the crime scene looks perfect. Which it normally does, it's usually any room. Perfect looking, it's not like there's often much blood or weapons. It's not scary….it's just this feeling. This awful feeling in my stomach'

'Are you uncomfortable?' Maria asked. Uncomfortable. That pit in my stomach. I thought about it….I was always bouncing my legs up and down more when I was interviewing in these cases. A co-worked had even said it to me. The lump in my throat that I felt before asking suspects questions wasn't something anyone else could notice but it was definitely something I felt more with this crime.

'Why would I be uncomfortable?" I asked, suddenly feeling slightly defensive despite the fact that she very well may be right. Maybe that was why I felt defensive. She knew me better than me.

'Well Sam, you went to college before joining the guards..' Maria turned to face me. 'One in five college students experience sexual assaults…majority female…if you break it down…

statistically you would have probably known people who sexually assaulted women…'

I sat up 'Maria…my friends didn't rape girls!'

'Sam, I'm not saying your friends did I'm just saying that maybe it makes you uncomfortable because as much as we're talking about it more, we still refuse to acknowledge how close to home it really is'

I sighed… I was angry. My friends, they couldn't, they wouldn't. People I knew…

Maria sighed and lay back 'we all find it very easy to think of someone we know that has been assaulted. We all do. I don't know anyone who doesn't know someone. But we never flip the coin, we don't speak about how if we all know someone who's been assaulted. Shouldn't we, just from a numbers point of view, also know someone who has assaulted another person'

I said nothing, her breathing slowly steadied so I knew she had fallen asleep. I tossed and turned. Many of my co-workers, especially the female ones, had at one point mentioned knowing someone who had been raped. How these cases made them even angrier. Because they were more relatable. But Maria was right. I was a man. If I knew of so many people being assaulted, I had definitely crossed paths with the people who did the assaulting. And I didn't mean the people I question in work. The people I pick up and interview and put away. I mean in my personal life too, in college, at parties, at lectures, on holidays. And the more I thought about it, the more I thought about those days and the words and the drink and the language. The more it scared me. How close we were to all of it. How…maybe we all were a part of it. It made me sick. I was scared of my little girls growing up, not because of what they would do but because of what could be done to them. And I was scared because I knew the way we had talked about and seen girls when we were younger.

No I had never hurt a girl, I knew that for sure. I also hoped none of my best friends had. Most of the guys I knew were really good guys but if I am being completely honest, maybe I contributed by never ever doing anything. I thought of how I had never ever chatted to a mate about sexual assault casually, but how Maria knew the exact statistic. Maria hadn't been sexually assaulted. As far as I knew. But it was a much bigger part of a woman's world.

We always say how inhuman it is, how awful that man must have been, how it is possibly the worst thing a person can do. We make the attacker this person that we think we would definitely know if we saw them. So vicious and uncaring and violent, but the truth is we wouldn't know a perpetrator if we saw them. They're walking among us every day. They have to be. That's why I was uncomfortable. The perpetrator was not the weird old man down the road who always looked out his window, or the teenager who had scary names in chat rooms and played terrifying metal music. No, the perpetrators were our classmates, the people who worked in the places we went to every day, they were someone's friend, someone's family, someone's boyfriend. The everyday perpetrators were us. The scariest part being, I had a sinking feeling that some of these perpetrators didn't even realize they were ones.

So yes, to say the least I was uncomfortable as I sat across from this young man and asked him about the party he was at.

'Yeah, it was my cousins party. It was Halloween night, as you know, and yeah I went by myself'

'By yourself?' I asked, writing down what he was saying.

'Yeah, well Liv's a bit younger than me. I didn't plan on staying long I was just dropping in to check in and make sure no one had burnt down my aunt's place yet'

'Liv is your cousins name?' I asked.

'Yeah, she's like best friends with Scarlett, who was also at the party which is the reason I'm here I'm guessing? Is she okay? Please tell me what's happened'

'Joel, can you tell me a bit about your relationship with Scarlett?'

'My relationship…what…we aren't in a relationship. We did date before a few years ago. But we broke up. That's all ages ago now though'

'Okay, how was Scarlett on the night of the 31st?' Alex asked.

Joe was quiet, he was looking down at his knees. 'Truthfully?' he asked from behind his hair.

'Yes completely truthfully Joel' I answered leaning back, Alex glanced at me sideways and straightened up in his chair.

'To be honest she was drunk, really drunk and Scarlett doesn't get drunk. I mean I think I've seen her tipsy once or twice'

'Did you see what she drinking?' asked Alex.

'No, I didn't actually see her drinking but she was babbling on about a bottle of wine and there was plenty of empty ones lying around…look I don't know…'

'Walk me through your night Joel, step by step' I asked

Joel sighed, he was shaking. A part of me felt sorry for him. If he had done nothing wrong this was a very frightening place to be in, I know even more frightening if he had done it but the fear of not being able to prove your innocence. I didn't know what the felt like but I knew what being a young lad felt like. The feigned confidence, the act of being nonchalant and unaffected. Pair this with the actual internal knowledge of realizing you know so little and feeling as though those around you must all be dealing with everything better because don't they look okay? I knew now that I was older that females had a different series of worries and anxieties at this age but I also only knew how it felt to be the guy.

Joel started to speak and I decided that I was going to listen to him with no bias.

'Okay, I arrived when a lot of people were already there. I saw Liv and Maddy straight away. They were in the living room. I started making my way towards them, I said hey and the usual....I don't really remember what we spoke about but Liv brought me to the fridge and got me a beer. Someone called her away, I was sort of looking for someone I recognized...I guess I was looking for Scarlett. But I wandered around the room, not recognizing many. I was standing when Scarlett came into the room with Bee, one of the other girls. I was almost thinking of leaving before I saw her...I guess I hadn't realized that I had sort of been wanting to see her... anyways sorry this is all irrelevant....

'No this is really helpful Joel, give us as many details as you can' Alex said, scribbling away.

I thought Joel was telling the truth because it wasn't easy to admit something like that. I was easier to have those little vulnerable thoughts race around your head and drive you crazy than to admit them to another. Especially to another two men. But then again, the magic show, he could be showing me something else to hide the other.

'Okay well, she was walking in with Bee, she looked drunk. I won't lie and say I didn't think that, but it was a party everyone was drunk. She came over to me. I didn't expect that, I guess I'm not sure what I expected....sorry off track...but yeah she came over. We chatted, we had lots to talk about I suppose, but it was all very general, nothing stands out. She then said she wanted another drink, so I think...yeah we walked over to the kitchen and she dropped her glass. I'm not sure if that was before or after she had a drink but I just remember we had to clean it up. Her friend…Bee, the one from earlier she helped'

Joel stopped. He looked as though he was making a decision in his mind. Like he was torn.

'Joel what is it?' I asked, following my gut.

'She was too drunk, I shouldn't have gone upstairs with her…. I should have left…or left her with Bee…she shouldn't have been alone'

'What happened upstairs Joel?' asked Alex, my stomach was turning. I don't know why but I didn't want this boy band look alike, young lad to have done this.

'So we went upstairs together, I don't actually know exactly what room we went into. But once we were in there I left to go to the bathroom, when I came back Scarlett was pretty much asleep. She seemed like she was going to get sick. I did try…I guess I wanted something to happen. I really did but she wasn't in any state so I said I would go get her some water…'

'When you say you did try Joel, what exactly do you mean?' I asked.

'I kissed her, but she kissed me back…my hands were on her but I didn't do anything I swear' he put his hands up 'I wouldn't I swear to god I wouldn't….she lay down and then she started to really fall asleep, she was mumbling and that's when I thought no I need to get her some water. But I really did think she would be okay after some water, I mean everyone can get a bit like that and then snap back out you know?'

Neither Alex nor I responded or reacted so Joel continued to speak.

'I told her I was going to go get some water and that's what I did. She was asleep on the bed or almost asleep and I shut the door behind her. I went downstairs, the party was still in full swing and I got a glass of water. But when I went back up she wasn't there. She was gone. I mean I had been a few minutes getting the water I supposed, I had bumped into a few guys I knew but...I didn't know where she had gone to but I did ask this guy who was on the landing...he wasn't really in a good state though. When I went back downstairs my cousin was crying, Maddy was with her and they told me that Scarlett was with David'

Alex and I exchanged a quick subconscious glance. Before quickly realizing we had and returning to looking at Joel. We knew it was David, or we know that Scarlett knew it was David. We just needed the full picture.

'David?' I asked, although we knew all this it was always a good thing when stories started to line up. Especially in these kind of cases. Where it was words and sentences in the right order from the right people that made the difference between a guilty verdict and a non-guilty verdict. It shouldn't be such a thin line that we walk, a verdict shouldn't be so fickle and changeable.

'I don't know who David was but it seemed like Maddy liked him but Scarlett was then kissing him. To be honest Scarlett was in no fit state when I left her for her to be kissing anyone. I know, I know I was going to be going back up to her...so maybe she had sobered up while I was gone but yeah...look that's all I know. I won't lie I was pissed off so I left, actually I was even more angry because some asshole wouldn't let me use the bathroom as I was leaving...but all of that seems silly now that I know that someone hurt Scarlett.'

'Okay Joel, do you remember anything else?" asked Alex, my heart was beating because of what Joel had said about the bathroom. Scarlett hadn't said anything about someone knocking but maybe she had been too out of it to have noticed. The injuries to her head were not reflective of a little bump. They were a bang. They were stitch worthy. They were evidence. Sam was thinking of how Joel could really help this case but only if he was telling the truth. Only if he told them everything.

'Anything else about the bathroom, what do you mean someone wouldn't let you in?' I asked, leaning forward. My muscles ached from sitting down all day, I thought about going home tonight. Would I be able to leave work at work or would I spend most of dinner downloading to Maria about this case like I ended up doing more often than not.

'Well I was leaving and I guess I was probably impatient because I was annoyed at the situation, annoyed at myself and Scarlett. But I banged on the door and presumed it was girls in there doing their usual girls stuff of chatting for years about whatever' he rolled his eyes 'but after no one replied and I heard nothing I knocked again and some guy shouted back basically telling me to fuck off. I don't know, he could have been doing drugs or something I didn't think much into it...why?"

'It's just important that we get as much details from the night that we can" said Alex, closing over his note book.

'Well I left then, I got a taxi, here I can even show you the time on the app. You can call the guy who was driving, he was telling me about his kid becoming a pilot' Joel reached into his pocket and took out his phone, he tapped a few times and held up his screen. It was a big Iphone so it wasn't hard to read from where we were sitting opposite him. On the screen was a little map at the top and underneath it had in the address I knew was Scarlett's home address and the time 00:55 and underneath another address which I would verify was Joel's with the time 01:13. The drivers name was at the bottom with an icon that said we could contact driver underneath.

'Could we take down these details?' asked Alex stretching his hand out to take the phone. Alex wrote down the details while Joel starred into his lap.

'What are you thinking Joel?' I asked slowly.

'I…is she okay? Can you tell me what happened because I really don't like what I've heard and… and she won't answer me and Liv said she's to leave her alone for a while and Liv won't even speak to me properly'

'We can't tell you what happened I'm afraid but I will say you have been very helpful. We will be in touch Joel and if you think of absolutely anything else from that night could you please contact us straight away. You know the number?'

Joel nodded. Alex handed him back his phone which he pocketed straight away.

'I do, okay.' He stood up and so did we.

'Thanks for coming in Joel' I said following him to the door and opening it for him. He just nodded.

I closed the door behind him and looked to Alex 'what do you think?' he asked.

'Maybe I shouldn't but I believe him, his story makes sense. I mean in a way it could have easily been him in David's position but it wasn't.'

'Hmm, you're right. But it does seem like David had a lot of aggression. I didn't see that in him but who knows'

'Scarlett knows' I said 'she knows it was David and she knows she had been with Joel beforehand. She is literally telling us exactly what we need…'

'We will still need more' said Alex 'David needs to tell us, it can't be just her word against his. Because we all know how that will go'

Kevin Stanley (Scarlett's Prosecution Solicitor)

"They say justice should equal truth but in reality, justice falls in favour of people who say exactly what society wants to hear'

I knew from the moment I laid eyes on Scarlett Love during our pretrial meeting that this case was going to be even harder than anticipated. It's a terrible thing to say but in my work, I have to try and look at my clients in the same way the jury would look at them and unfortunately, I knew exactly what they would see. See Scarlett Love is a beautiful young girl, she is small and slim. She isn't even your average pretty girl, she is striking. Objectively speaking she is absolutely beautiful and no one could deny that. Not that it should matter. But the last thing she looks like is a victim. Her eye are piercing, her gaze is strong, she holds herself extremely well and her manner is powerful, she does not come across as a meek timid seventeen-year-old. She does not look like she is possible of being a victim. But the worst thing about my work is that people judge far too quickly on what they see.

Sexual assault cases are my main line of work because I want to try and change the way our society views and acts upon the crime. Scarlett Love was, in my eyes and only if we lived in an ideal fair world, the perfect client. She was brave, mature beyond her years but most of all she was honest, and as much as I appreciated and wanted more of her honesty in the world, I feared for how the jury would judge her for it. They say justice should equal truth but in reality, justice falls in favour of people who say exactly what society want to hear. They want something that is easy for them to hear, to understand, to come to terms with. Even if it is not the actual truth. They want a nice truth. They want to be able to sleep soundly at night. No-one wants to think the people they know could be capable of such violent acts, but this is too common of an act for us to not know someone who perpetrates it.

In our very first meeting she laid down all the facts for me

'I know you'll have read my case in detail obviously and all of that, but I want you to know me for me and not for what has happened to me recently'

I nodded slowly, curious and urging her to continue.

'People have been saying a lot of things about me, I know that, I see it online…my little sister hears in in school….my parents have been getting letters. I know people think I'm a slut….all these guys are now defending David, saying stuff that I have done with them before. It wouldn't be the same way if I was a guy…if I was a guy I would be getting praised for having been with girls…I wouldn't be getting slut shames.

But I want to be clear that none of that matters…or it shouldn't and I need to know that you're on my side with that. I need to know that you also agree. That those words and whispers, that they have absolutely nothing, nothing to do with the fact that I was….that I was assaulted." she took a deep breath. Her hands were shaking. I knew she had more than likely rehearsed more in her head but the saying out loud of it was challenging… 'They're two separate… they're two completely separate things'

I admired her. I knew boys, I had been one myself obviously, and in many ways I still was. And I had grown up with five older brothers. The things boys would say about girls could sometimes be so cruel, absolutely sickening. Even though most of it was all what they call locker room talk, which shouldn't even be a thing. And it is true that many of the boys who spoke this way would never act in the way they spoke. But speaking about something makes it more acceptable. But Scarlett was so right. People would call her a slut, and not only boys, girls could also be cruel. For some reason we had all become conditioned to judge. She was also right about the fact that a boy wouldn't be being called a slut for doing the same things as a woman. I I am well aware that a boy who has a lot of sex is not a slut but a hero. This is all common knowledge, this is all something we've heard many times before, yet it is still something we are failing to destigmatize….it is something that unfortunately our society has come to accept. Boys will be boys and girls will be….nice?

I clasped my hands together. 'I fully agree with you Scarlett, and I'm really glad you told me that….' I took a deep breath 'but unfortunately this sort of attitude comes up in nearly every case. From the defence I mean, this attitude of shaming the victim. Of judging the persons character. I mean, if we were to go into court taking the angle of saying my past doesn't matter – it is a separate thing etc etc..it would be a massive risk because as much as that is the world we want, it is not the world we live in. It is not the ideal world that the court lives in either…does that make sense? I wish I could say that we could go in with that and we could change people's attitudes but if we actually want to win the case we are better off not challenging the jury too much. I really hope you know that isn't my own personal opinion though, I personally would love to hear the real truth in a court room"

Scarlett nodded 'I thought as much, I mean I'm not completely naïve but a part of me just… a part of me is too hopeful maybe…'

'Scarlett, I promise you right now, I am going to try my very best. I have full faith in you, in us as a team. I really believe we can do this.'

Scarlett was quiet. Biting her lips.

'What are you thinking?' I asked gently.

'I'm...I'm thinking that I've made a mistake...but I think that ten times a day so I suppose it's nothing new hey...' she seemed lost. The way she held herself could make you forget that she was only a kid, only a young woman who had gone through such a brutal act of violation. Of course she was scared, she must be terrified.

'It's normal to be scared, to be terrified. But you're being so brave, go easy on yourself not a lot of people could do what you're doing now...'

'Kevin I don't really feel like I have a choice, I know that sounds weird...of course I have a choice... but as scared as I am of going through with this, the idea of not doing anything, it terrifies me. I don't know if I'd ever sleep again. Maybe I never will regardless...but right now, right now this is all I have'

I nodded. I liked Scarlett, she was sort of slightly intimidating in mannerisms. She gave the impression of being self-assured but as I got to know her I saw that she was being what she thought she needed to be. And she was probably right. The court wasn't a level playing field, you couldn't go in being yourself and being authentic and hope for the best. You had to know the rules, you had to be in the know. Scarlett and I spoke some more, she wanted to make a victim impact statement so long as David wasn't in the room. This could be arranged. I went through the process with her, I was glad she was doing this because it was literally one of the few elements to the trial that generally worked in the favour of the victim. The jury find it harder when they hear them speak directly about the effects of a crime as opposed to just hearing a crime played out like it is just in a crime documentary. It's more real.

'I'll just write what I know…I don't know how it's going to have affected me in the future yet Kevin…'

'I know, just write about what it is doing now, what your fearful of for the future…about school and how you're not going. Your family and the different sort of trauma you can see now'

Scarlett looked at me. She had a look in her eyes I couldn't quite pinpoint but it unsettled me. There was a sort of wantonness to it, a wildness I couldn't understand.

'Yes Kevin. I'll write what I know' she said again before getting up. I nodded 'Thanks Scarlett…I'll see you soon' she just nodded as she left. There was certainly something about that young woman…I thought this could go very strongly in either direction but her faith and my gut told me we were doing the right thing. That regardless of outcome, this right now was the right thing. I couldn't get the look in her eyes out of my mind though.

Samantha

"A woman who cried too much or gave out too much, they don't want that'

I knocked on my sisters door. Never in my life had I gone to Scarlett's door as much as I had in the last few months. Scarlett didn't spend this much time in her room. Scarlett was always 'I'm gone for a quick run I'll be back by dinner' and out she would race into the cold, earphones in. Or Scarlett was downstairs, making Toblerone cheesecake, causing havoc in the kitchen. Or she was in dad's office, asking him endless questions until he eventually would cry out 'Scarlett please' and she would scuffle off. Or if it was a weekend and mum was home, she was out to her in the garden, where she would try and pot a plant but end up covered in soil. Mum would sigh 'Scarlett they were my hydrangeas can you...can you please just put that down' Scarlett wasn't a room person in the way I was. I loved my room, my favourite thing after a day of school was to come home and lie on my emerald green fluffy duvet, put on a podcast and avoid my homework and responsibilities until Scarlett came in and lay beside me. We would discuss the school day, I would complain about having too much maths and not enough time to do art, Scarlett would complain about how silly doing subjects we hated was even though she didn't really mind any, we would practise our bed tumbles and our hair flicks, laughing as we would fall off the end on to my carpeted floor. Scarlett would play me her new favourite songs for running, I would show her a new Instagram page I found. Scarlett would tell me about Liv and Bee and Maddy. I'd tell her about Clara and any of the current boy drama. In reality, these usually lasted between ten and fifteen minutes. The time between getting home from school and having dad call us down for dinner. But when I think of Scarlett and me. I think of my bed, with her and me on it. I think of how safe it was, how I could tell her anything. How there was never a bad moment on that duvet. In reality we lay there and we did nothing, but to me, it was everything. Now Scarlett was always in her room when I came home, she studied the endless pages of her own life. Just in case she would use a different turn of phrase to describe the same two minutes, that couldn't happen. Or she was reading articles, statistics, trying to remain calm, cool, collected. When I knocked on her door, I wanted to hear Scarlett screaming on the other side of the door. But I knew she was just sitting at her desk, earphones in. Every single person that we'd come across, from solicitors and lawyers and representatives and peoples who's job I didn't even understand what it was, had told Scarlett 'try your best to stay calm honey, stay calm and collected when you're in that court. When you're in public, when you're asked questions' The court didn't want to see an angry woman, a woman who lost her temper couldn't be reliable witness. A woman who cried too much or gave out too much, they don't want that. Calm, cool, collected. The newspapers can't write about what an emotional wreck you are if you don't show any emotion okay?

'Come in' I heard from the other side of the door.

Scarlett was lying on her tummy on her bed, re-reading her victim impact statement. I knew it was this because it was in bright pink, she'd read that this would help it stay in her memory better.

'Wanna go for a run?' I asked, sitting down next to her.

She looked up at me and gave me a look 'A run? Babe you don't run' she laughed a little.

'Well…I could learn, you could teach me, it can't be that hard. I'm pretty good at walking' I smiled and Scarlett hit me softly, messing.

'I don't know little one…' she sighed turning over onto her back.

'Come on Scarlett, you're stuck in here all day. Let's run, we can go to the back track in the park. We won't meet anyone there'

Scarlett continued to look at the ceiling.

'Please Scarlett…for me' I added in cheekily.

'You are so bold, alright come on then, get your stuff on and be downstairs in 3 minutes. No messing around we are running 5k at least'

'I love you' I said as I raced out. 5km though…..the last time I had run was when Clara left her brand new phone on the 46A bus and realized just as we got off. Even at that she was the one who kept running…I stopped and shouted encouragement.

Three and half minutes later Scarlett closed the front door behind us. She looked not scared but shook.

'Let's warm up' I said, bending forward to touch my toes.

'Okay if we go around that back route twice we will have done just under 5km door to door okay Sam?'

I nodded and she started to jog. I ran after her.

Within minutes I was puffed but I was so happy to have Scarlett next to me, and I was happy that for the first time in ages it wasn't next to me on the couch or in bed. I had been sleeping with her recently. Sometimes she would wake with a bolt, you know the way it sometimes happen when you wake in the middle of a dream or nightmare. That happened a few times a night. Sometimes she put her hands up randomly. I wondered what she would be like now if she hadn't told anyone, or if she had only told me. would I still be sleeping with her every night, surely she would at least have to be in school more because she wouldn't have given a reason to not be. It wouldn't be public knowledge. Would she be able…

'Nanny Lola' Scarlett said, through her breath as she ran next to me.

'What?' I asked breathlessly, trying to match her pace. She slowed down slightly.

'Nanny Lola told me…a few years ago…she told me that when she was younger her boyfriend used to rape her'

'What?' I stopped but Scarlett kept running so I sprinted to catch up with her 'Scarlett what?'

'It's why I have to keep doing this Sam, it's why I had to tell people. Nanny Lola didn't…and she said it ate her up inside. Think of how much it must have…" Scarlett took a breath 'how much it must have affected her if she was still thinking about it in her eighties'

'When…how did she tell you?' I asked panting at this stage but distracted.

'When I started dating Joel, I was so obsessed I would talk to Nanny Lola about him all the time and she told me….she wanted me to be careful, that even the people we love and are blinded by can have an alternative side to them…'

'She was right' I said 'I miss her'

'I miss her too…but this…this would have broke her heart' said Scarlett as we began our second lap.

I couldn't argue with that. But poor Nanny Lola…and Scarlett knowing this.

'Do mum and dad know?' I asked

'No, god no, and you mustn't tell them, Nanny trusted me. I just, I wanted at least one person to understand why I am doing this…I wanted there to be one person who doesn't think I'm crazy'

'Not everyone thinks that you're crazy Scarlett, people believe you'

Scarlett was silent.

'I know what you mean though, I won't tell anyone' I breathed out.

'Thanks Sam, I just was so afraid….I don't want to be eighty and have this hanging over me. Nanny Lola got out but it followed her. I love her so much but I couldn't do the same....she wouldn't have wanted it either"

'She knows' I said 'she knows and she's so proud'

Scarlett grinned at me 'You little hippy you been talking to her have you?'

I smiled, well used to her teasing of my beliefs, of my thoughts that she was all around us always.

'You know what I mean, oh Jesus Scarlett can we be done soon I think I might collapse'

'You won't collapse you drama queen, we've 1km left you can do this'

I grimaced and made a face at her but I kept going. The pounding of our two feet in unison was comforting in a strange way. It was going forward. We were moving forward. I thought about how everything could go wrong, but I would always have Scarlett and she would always have me. It started to rain.

'Scarlett seriously' I cried out

'The faster you run the quicker we're dry!' she picked up the pace.

'I hate you' I shouted after her, attempting to catch up. She would always be strides ahead of me. But she was my big sister. That's the way it was.

'Come on Sam you got this' she shouted back and for the first time she was smiling with the spark that Scarlett had always had. As if she had forgotten what was going on. I ran faster. As her little sister I might never fully catch up with Scarlett but I would make it my mission to make sure she never lost that spark again.

David (the accused)

The way I'd started to see it was that I was a result of a systematic failing and not simply my own failing. What happened that halloween night was a direct reflection of the society I grew up in and what I was accustomed to. We are an accumulation of our experiences and who we know and meet and this is how I have ended up where I am today. This was what my therapist and I were talking about this week. He suggested that I was perhaps avoiding any accountability 'I'm not suggesting you are guilty David, I'm only saying that we are here to talk about you and the role that you played in this event. We are not here to discuss the actions of others, in order for our work to be beneficial to you we need to be focusing on your actions. Yes the actions of others can impact us, so can their words but only we can take responsibility for what we do'

I wasn't particularly fond of my therapist. Sid was his name which I thought was a childish name for a grown man. Especially a grown man who went around trying to help people better themselves. A 'Sid' didn't sound like he knew a whole lot about the world but my Sid did. Although I wasn't fond of him I couldn't fault him. If I did have any other problems in my life that maybe made me feel sad or down as opposed to this, which just made me feel utterly and overwhelmingly confused I would probably come to him.

Actually, that's a lie, I would never have ever dreamed of saying the words "I go to therapy" because what idiots go to therapy. But now that I had to actually be there, well my mum and dad were forcing me, I would be lying if I didn't say it was sort of okay. Sid had an ease about him and a complete lack of judgement. Even when he was telling me to take accountability he was saying it in such a way that didn't sound like someone giving out to me or judging me.

'I don't want to take accountability for something I didn't do – I didn't rape Scarlett, I don't know how many times I'm going to have to say the same thing over and over' I sighed, exasperated. I was sick of this.

'Okay David, so what did you do then? Why are we here?' asked Sid.

'We're here because I had sex with a drunk girl and she has now decided she didn't want that to happen"

Sid just looked back at me. Silence. This guy got one hundred euro an hour to spend seventy percent of an hour in silence. I should become a therapist. I wasn't going to give in this time though, Sid would usually wait until I felt uncomfortable and then I would speak more but no, not this time.

'Tell me that again David' Sid finally said. I sighed.

'We're here because….because I had sex with a drunk girl..' I paused 'fuck it, I know that's not great but it's normal, we're here because this drunk girl changed her mind. This girl wanted to ruin my life'

'And what do you make of that?' Sid asked.

'What do I? What?' I responded.

'Well what can you take from that, how can you understand that?" Sid repeated.

'I can…I can understand that I wish I could go back and not do it. I wish I could have….' I didn't know what to say. I didn't know what I wished could happen.

'What would you do in that situation now, if you were back there?" Sid asked.

I wanted to say that I wouldn't have gone near Scarlett, I wanted that to be true. But I was smarter than that. I knew I would have gone near Scarlett – why wouldn't I? She was hot, she was fun, we'd hung out. I wanted to have sex with her. I didn't want this to happen but I had wanted her.

But Sid didn't want to hear that.

'I wouldn't go near her' I lied and then thought better of my lie as I saw Sid's normally neutral face react.

'Okay no, I would probably talk to her but I guess I would recognise now that she was more drunk than she should be…Sid I don't get how this is helpful, I can't change it' I took a sip of the glass of water that was always next to me in this room. In this low lit room. My mum would be waiting outside in the car, she never even left when she dropped me her, she just sat. It was like her life had nothing in it apart from looking after me. It was so boring to watch.

'What are you thinking about David?' asked Sid, he must have noted my vacant expression.

'My mum' I said truthfully. Sid was silent.

'My whole life it's like…..it's like her world has revolved around us. Around me and Millie and I just…I feel bad about it but…I don't know..i feel weirdly angry at her for it…"

'Angry?' asked Sid

'Well it's just so typical isn't it….such a typical life…she had kids, she looked after them, she works a little, dad is the one who actually has an interesting life. Her life was babies and school runs and activities…I don't know I'm getting…I don't know why I'm talking about this…' I trailed off.

'It's the connections our brains make David, it's actually important to note what comes up for you when we talk about the incident with Scarlett because sub-consciously we are associating other events and feelings in our life with it" Sid responded, leaning forward slightly.

'I guess...I guess I would never really....I don't know, be in awe or like want to be like my mum in the same way I would want to be like my dad...even with what's going on now. Like mum is just so...so annoyingly supportive, it's like she's walking on eggshells around me now. Whereas dad, he's straight with me. He tells me what to do, what to say, he doesn't try and talk about feelings or about how things will be okay, how I am actually a good person...he doesn't try that"

Silence again.

'There's just something I have for my dad that I don't have for my mum and I don't know what it is...'

'What does it feel like?' asked Sid. Feelings again, he was becoming like my mother now.

'It feels like a mix of anger and annoyance and just a sort of frustration but I love her, I love her of course...I just....' I couldn't find the right word. I couldn't place exactly what it was that I didn't have for my mum but it was something.

'There's something missing' I said 'but I don't get why that's linked to Scarlett any everything there...I don't think it is'

Sid nodded. 'I think we will wrap it up there for today then David, but keep thinking and remember that the associations we make aren't unrelated okay?'

I nodded and stood up.

'See you next week' I said, letting myself out. I walked down the hallway, past the two people waiting to see their listeners. I never actually wondered much as to why they were here. They were the same faces, same time, every week without fail. I wondered if they thought about why I was here, what they'd think if they knew I had been accused of raping someone and that's why I needed some dude to analyse me every week. When I walked outside my mums car was exactly where she had let me out. Of course it was. I got in.

'How'd it go?' she asked. She always asked this, she always asked it softly and kindly and always handed me a VitHit. I took the bottle off her.

'All fine' I said shortly 'let's just go home'. I didn't know why I was like this with her. Mum started to drive. She turned on the radio. I looked out the window, I didn't like the pit in my stomach that my session with Sid had left me with. I didn't like not knowing what I was feeling, I didn't like that I was afraid to know what I was feeling. I looked over to my mum, she had her usual furrowed brow expression. I realized what I didn't feel for my mother, and I hated myself for it but as soon as I realized the word it felt like the right fit for my emotions towards her. It was what I had for my dad, for my friends, for others but not for my mum. It was respect.

Maddy (Scarlett's best friend)

"Every minute worldwide someone is raped. Every minute. I can't believe I didn't know this. I can't believe I wasn't taught this"

'I think we'd be the two best hostesses" Scarlett said, pouring some ice into the two mugs of coffee we had in front of us. I took two metal straws out of her kitchen drawer and stuck them in.

'We really would, it would have to be a package deal though wouldn't it?' I said, taking a sip. 'more sugar'

Scarlett handed me the white bag and I put in another full spoonful.

'Oh of course, like you can't hire her without me and vice versa. Sell ourselves as working best as a team'

'Emirates would be fools to not have us' I smiled. 'I really just don't feel like I'll be ready for college Scar, I'm so afraid'

'You'd be amazing Mads, whatever you decide to do, you would smash it'

It was only a few weeks into 6th year and already questions were flying around of what we were all going to put on our CAO, where we wanted to go, who we wanted to be. I knew who I wanted to be, I wanted to be with Scarlett, with Liv and Bee.

'That's the problem, I have absolutely no idea. I don't even know if like anything at all in school, no scratch that, I know that don't like anything in school' we laughed.

'Air hostesses it is so, we'll find our calling somewhere over the Atlantic I'm sure"

'Look it doesn't seem like I'm finding it here anyways' I said and Scarlett laughed.

A few weeks later Scarlett was raped, and it would be at least a year before we spoke again about our dreams for when we left school.

Since the moment I was in London and heard from Liv about what had happened to Scarlett I had been driven crazy by a need to know as much as I could about sexual assault. In that moment I felt so guilty, so guilty for having been angry and annoyed at Scarlett. I also felt a strange conflict thought because I suppose I was a bit jealous of Scarlett. She was my best friend in this life, I loved her as much as I had loved anyone, but I still envied the way she took life in her stride. The way nothing phased her and the way she was completely and unapologetically herself. But once Liv called me, I freaked out. I cried to my mum and once she heard that Scarlett had reported and I texted Scarlett who didn't respond straight away but her little sister called me and explained everything, I called the team they said was working on her case. I called them and I told them that David took her away, headed towards the bathroom. I hated myself that I hadn't registered that she was too drunk, I had been blinded by my jealousy and I can't even say those words out loud to her. I can't believe I'd been trying to get with this man, I couldn't believe he had done this to her, it was much easier to not believe. But I knew Scarlett, and I know that my mum has always told me that you never ever really know anyone, and I do agree with her, but I just don't believe that Scarlett would lie or embellish anything like this. Now that I know everything that I know, I believe that very few people out there would. It's not worth it.

When I came back to school after our week off, our whole world had tilted. There was a divide. Me, Liv and Bee had promised each other that we would stick together through it all, regardless, and that we would say very little about Scarlett. But word has spread like wildfire, when we opened our lockers notes flew out. I thought that sort of child play only happened in American teen movies. I was so wrong.

'Scarlett's a whore'

'Lying bitch'

'You know your best friends a total slut right'

'Do you all have sex with everyone too?'

'You can't just change your mind'

'I don't...' started Bee picking up a few that had flown out of her locker from the ground.

'This is actually ridiculous, their making it look like this is some kind of joke. This is not a fucking joke I hate this' Liv said, snatching the notes off me and off Bee. She shoot death stares around us, no one had spoken to us yet this morning. I had guessed it might be like this for a little while but I hadn't really known what it would feel like. I didn't like this, I felt sick in my stomach. For a brief moment, I wished we hadn't been Scarlett's best friends.

Liv slammed her locker shut. 'Liv, people are staring...' whispered Bee. I looked around, she wasn't wrong. It wasn't overly obvious but people were hanging around. The guys mainly. The guys who were so unafraid of anything. I was furious but I was scared. Liv however showed no fear.

'I don't care Bee' she spun around 'alright guys, got a problem? Say it to us instead of being a literal five year old child and writing it on a piece of paper!' Liv was shouting now, at no one in particular but just out loud. I had never ever seen her like this, I didn't know she could be like this.

'Whore' shouted a voice from down the hallway, an eruption of laughter followed. Liv threw her bag down.

'Who the fuck said that?' she shouted turning around.

'Liv wait' I said, grabbing her arm just as our maths teacher turned the corner towards us, blocking our view from down the hallway.

'Olivia Locke, what is going on?" asked Mrs. O'Connell 'did I just hear you shouting?'

'Mrs, we're sorry we…'Liv cut Bee off

'We're not sorry Mrs, the boys are harassing us and they're… their literally making what happened to Scarlett into a joke.. it's…' Liv wasn't breathing properly.

'It's okay, it's okay' I said facing her 'here breath with me' she was starting to have a panic attack. Liv hadn't had one in years, since when her sister was sick and she would freak out. I held her hands as she started to kneel towards the ground. I sat opposite her as Bee spoke quietly to Mrs. O'Connell. Once Liv had returned to normal breath and pace, she looked up to Mrs. O'Connell.

'Come with me girls' she said softly reaching her hand out for Liv who took it. Bee took mine and we followed Liv and our maths teacher, hand in hand. We knew our days at school we're never going to be the way the were the week beforehand.

'We've got to be older than we feel is what my mum told me' said Bee softly, as we sat in the schools reception. Waiting for the guidance counsellor to come out to us. I didn't even know we really had one of them.

I nodded. 'Things are going to really change' said Liv. Mrs. O'Connell came back out 'want to come in for a chat ladies?"

'I think our worlds already have' I said softly to the girls as we all stood up.

Change isn't not happening because sexual assault isn't common or not happening or not something we need to worry about or change. Change is not happening because in order for change to happen we need to take accountability for our action or perhaps the better way to say it is, we need to take accountability for our lack of action. We need to acknowledge our ignorance. We need to take accountability. This is what I have learned by becoming engrossed in this world, I taught myself stuff in order to feel safer, I taught myself as much as I could to feel better for Scarlett, to feel stronger for her.

Sexual assault is an epidemic. Not something that happens that we don't talk about. It is inspiring and amazing to see the way our incredible world can come together and take action in times of crisis and for major issues across the world, but why are we continuing to ignore the epidemic that is happening to someone every minute. Every minute worldwide someone is raped. Every minute. I can't believe I didn't know this. I can't believe I wasn't taught this. I can list you the periodic table in order but I didn't have any facts or figures about sexual assault taught to me? I didn't have any idea what consent really was until recently. With someone being raped every minute we can't say that it's not something that we all have to try and change. But first accountability, and accountability is hard because accountability means acknowledging that we haven't been doing enough. That maybe we have laughed at jokes that aren't funny. Accountability means taking responsibility for what we have done wrong. But the trickiest part to this is that if we are going to take responsibility and accountably we are going to have to then start to actively try and be better. We can't take responsibility and then not change a thing. And change is scary, change involves being disliked by those who aren't ready for your change or who aren't ready for change themselves.

Una (David's mother)

"This was my sacrifices and my rewards."

This was my years and years of work and tears and unconditional love and maybe this was the biggest test I would have'

When my son was seven years old he came in the back door crying. His school backpack was almost bigger than him and with his shoulders shrugged it was dragging behind him.

'Darling, what's wrong?' I had asked, turning off my laptop and placing my reading glasses on top of my head. I stood up.

'They called me a girl' he said, a teardrop rolling down his face.

'What do you mean honey?' I took his backpack off his back and he flung his little arms around my waist. 'Shh it's alright, what happened David?"

'The ball hit me...' he let out a little sob 'it hit me and it hurt and I cried cause it hurt and Luke and Scott...they laughed'

I placed me hands on his shoulders and kneeled down in front of me

'But that's okay David, if it hurt it's okay to cry. When things hurt we all cry' I said

'But they said I was acting like a little girl, like Millie' he pointed a finger across the room at his four year old sister who was sitting silently on a beanbag. Earphones in, thumb being sucked, Millie was engrossed in her own little world of Peppa Pig or whatever animal it was that was talking on her screen. She hadn't so much as looked up when her brother entered the kitchen.

'Well Millie is not a bad way to be now so she's not – '

'Yes, yes she is, they make fun of people who cry and girls cry always' he cried out, plonking himself down at the kitchen table.

'That's not true David, everyone can cry' I sighed as I sat down opposite my little boy.

'I don't care I don't want to be called a girl' his hand reached over the table a took a banana from the bowl in the middle.

'That wasn't very nice of them was it?' I said softly, just wanting my son to not be upset. Wanting him to feel loved and seen. David munched his banana and looked back at me. his cheeks puffy from crying and tear marks around his eyes. He shook his head.

As I ironed my now nineteen year old son's shirt; I wished I had told him that the insult wasn't being told he was acting like a girl. That in fact that should have been a compliment and not an insult. That the real problem was not him crying at all but really was that the other boys didn't know it wasn't right to use the phrase cry like a girl. But then again, did I ever tell my own son to not use this phrase.

I wondered how we'd got here. Tomorrow my son would stand in that courtroom wearing the shirt that I pressed the iron into right now. Tomorrow he would say he wasn't guilty and he would talk about his version of the night. Tomorrow I would hear it all, again and again and again.

My son was a child that I still felt responsible for. I still felt as though his actions were indirectly my actions. I couldn't believe that he had done what this girl said he had done. Because then really, wasn't I to blame? I would much rather have the blame on me than him but unfortunately it was not me who was on trial. Even if it did feel that way at times. I had spoken to barely anyone but my sister and husband. In the last few months my world had become very small.

My husband walked into the living room where I was 'hey' he said softly, touching my hips gently and standing next to me.

'How is he?' I asked as he sat down on the couch.

'Much the same' Ryan sighed, running had hands through his greying hair. I flattened out the shirt and turned off the iron.

'I'm so afraid Ryan' I said as I sank down next to him 'what's going to happen to him?"

'it's a misunderstanding Una, this is our David we're talking about. Our David Una' he looked at me. I knew what he was saying. This was what we had accomplished with our lives. David. David was our biggest and greatest achievement, how could I be questioning that.

'What's he doing?' I asked quietly

'We had a chat, I told him to just do exactly what the lawyers have said. To not give anything extra or hold back anything that's already known. He says he's trying to sleep now, he needs it Una he hasn't slept for more than three hours in I don't know how long'

I was silent. David was our eldest child. It had taken us a long time to have him. And then Millie came along shortly after. She was the one who had caused us much more stress, she was unpredictable and erratic, but she loved fiercely and had a heart larger than anyone I knew. She has been so torn up since this happened, I genuinely think she feels physically torn. She has been staying with my sister and her kids for the last few weeks. Things were getting too much at school, being the sister of the accused.

I thought of what we had done that had led to this. I couldn't shake Scarlet's face from my mind. I didn't really know the girl at all before any of this happened and now I knew more about her and my sons sexual relations than any mother would ever want to know. What I couldn't get out of my head was that if I knew what I knew about their encounter, what did her mother know. What was her mother's version of events. Because that's what we had in common, what all mothers had in common, we loved our child more than anything in this world and we would defend them until the end. Sometimes it felt like I was in battle with myself. With another version of me.

'Are you going to be okay tomorrow?" Ryan asked me. I thought for a moment.

'I don't know how to answer that…' I replied 'are you going to be okay?' I asked back.

Ryan sighed 'me too, I don't know. But we have to be, for David okay? We have to be okay'

I nodded. I had never been an angry person. I was a pre-school teacher, I was quiet and soft spoken and more often than not afraid of my own shadow. I had never felt anger before David told me about that night. Yet I couldn't pinpoint who I was angry at, first I was angry at him, then I was angry at myself, then my husband for not educating him more on what was supposed to be his man to man talks, I was angry at the girl, I was angry at the system that created a world where this happened.

But I was also so upset for him, for the two of them. For the path that him and Scarlett were now on and how it was going to affect the rest of their lives.

I had sat David down when we got back from his first questioning at the guards.

'David, I need you to tell me exactly what happened and I need you to tell me it all. Whatever it is, however bad it is I will support you until the end but I can't support you properly if I don't know what happened'

David had tears in his eyes, his dad was still on his way home so for now it was just the two of us.

'David I love you so much and nothing will ever change that okay? But you need to tell me everything so I can help you'

'I didn't think it was that bad mum. I really don't think I am guilty of what she says I did. I had sex with her yes' he threw his hand up, he was exasperated. He got like this, as did most teenage boys when they couldn't verbalise what was running through their mind.

'Okay but how did it happen. Tell me why she could think this was rape?' I asked as he ran his hands through his hair.

'She was drunk' he said 'I was drunk too though, and it's not like she hasn't done it before' I made sure my face remained neutral, I needed to hear it all however difficult it was.

'But yeah I was angry and I probably took it too far but she would have had sex with me anyways. If not that night then another night, she's just annoyed that she was drunk and she was upset over some other guy and I think everything's just gotten all mixed up'

'Why were you angry?" I asked gently

'Because she was acting drunk and I knew I knew she would have been fine if she were sober. I was taking care of her, I was making sure she didn't embarrass herself in front of everyone. I...I didn't rape her mum'

'Okay...' I started slowly 'David did you two have a conversation before sex or during it or...' my stomach felt sick and I couldn't believe I was asking my eighteen year old son these questions but I was and I was going to keep asking them until I understood what happened. Until I figured out why that girl had left that party feeling assaulted and attacked and my son left feeling as though he had simply had sex.

He sighed. 'No, no we didn't and yes I know I should have but no one actually does that. I know that's what they say to do but no one does it. Everyone just knows, that would just be awkward in so many ways...and I mean she's come on to me before ....' his voice trailed off

'David, I have to ask you and it's not me not believing you or accusing you of anything but it's what you're going to be asked' I swallowed...the scratch above your eye David...?'

'For fuck's sake' he put his head on the table 'it's a tiny scratch...' his voice was rising

'David' I said calmly 'you just need to explain it to me'

'She scratched me okay? Are you happy, she fucking scratched me and because she fucking scratched me I'm going to be suddenly called a rapist? No, guys get scratched all the time during sex, sorry mum, but seriously, our backs and shoulders and no that's fucking ridiculous that just because she simply scratches me means she can take it all back. Did you see what she was wearing? I know I shouldn't say that but I mean she's Scarlett, she's always up for it I don't understand why it's my life she's choosing to ruin'

I stayed silent. Parts of what my own son had just said made me so angry but they also made me acutely aware of the attitudes of eighteen year old males and I knew this from when I was young too. In an alternative world where we all were actually respected and not just pretended to be maybe I would have stood up and shouted but I wasn't in that world. I had stood up too many times as a teenager and been spoken over that I was now afraid to stand up to my own son?

'I'm not guilty, maybe she thinks what happened was rape but to me it was sex, and yes she was drunk and yes maybe I should have been a bit.....gentler or something but no way am I a rapist. No way. That's not how this works. I was drunk too, how come it's her excuse but can't be mine?' He looked up at me, he was crying. I put my hand over his hand.

'Okay David' I said, 'I believe you'

And in all honesty I wasn't lying. I believed that he truly thought what had happened wasn't rape. I believed that he thought he was telling the truth. And really was it his fault for not being educated? Was that not supposed to be me who taught him right from wrong? Who taught him that he should never ever use what a woman wears as a tool against her? Shouldn't he know better? I couldn't deal with what I thought my son should be, respectful, kind, aware. What I hoped he would be. I could only deal with who was sitting in front of me, that was the son that I had. This was my son. This was my sacrifices and rewards. This was my years and years of work and tears and unconditional love and maybe this was the biggest test I would have. I didn't have the time to process what this would mean for me, what this made me feel like, how would this impact how I viewed myself. I didn't have time for that because after giving birth to David my roles switched from being Una first, to suddenly being always a mother first and my own person second. I wasn't sure if this was right, I never asked my mum this in those words I guess. But it was how I felt.

So right now after my husband asked me if I would be okay, I realized it didn't matter yet. Maybe the time would never come when it did matter. What mattered was David and how he was going to survive this and come out the other end. Mum first, Una second.

5

The Trial

Scarlett

*'A woman's word is first doubted before it is believed and there is something
so fundamentally wrong in that'*

I looked up at the jury's faces. I felt like I could read their minds and I didn't like what I saw. They doubted me, their eyes said it all. My case was pushing the limit, this I knew from the get go, but perhaps I had too much faith in humanity. Or maybe I was naïve. Whatever I was, they had given up on me already, after hearing everything he had said.

I cleared my throat, I adjusted the hem of my dress. The court was completely silent, waiting for me to speak. My victim impact statement. My last chance to convince them that no matter what I did or who I was, I didn't deserve this.

'I' I started shakily; my voice hoarser then I'd imagined. It had never been so hard to articulate the words my mind was screaming. I had wrote this down, in every colour ink. I'd read somewhere that green ink stayed in your mind the most but then I read somewhere else that red did that. I didn't know which to believe so I did every colour, I had the printed black print version in front of me but I hadn't trusted myself to be able to read properly while I was up here. I wanted to know this by heart.

'I...' I tried again. I shook my head and looked straight to the jury.

'My name is Scarlett Love. I am not perfect. I am a very normal eighteen year old. I never thought I would have to say these words but I'm not a saint.....I'm not pretending to be... because but at the end of the day, who is?' they looked at me. They stared blankly back, I could feel the tears prickling but now was not the time. Now was the time to be braver. Now was the time to do the hard things. I was at a loss for the words on my sheet and my eyes were blurred. I carried on, momentarily forgetting that I had spent hours analysing the right collection of words, and just going for what I felt like saying.

'I' I continued, searching for the right words. I lost track of where I was going with this. I wanted the words. The simplest words. 'Okay, that is not what this should be about. It should not be a good girl bad girl trial. It should not be a case of who I am as a person. Throughout this process I forgot, I forgot that I was actually not the accused one. I was actually, believe it or not, the one who's character should not be on 'trial'. Yet It felt like I was the one who needed to prove myself, as if I was the perpetrator. I needed to be an angel in order for everyone to believe that I was....what, innocent? In a crime that was committed against me?. I forgot that I was not guilty. Because that is what you feel when this happens to you. You feel guilty. I feel guilty, I feel ashamed. You wonder, I constantly wonder what I could have done differently. I didn't need people questioning my every move, I was already questioning my every move. What he did to me, is always with me. This trial, will always be with me. I was asked to write this statement to try and explain how this has affected me. The truth is that this has affected me in ways that words cannot express, and unfortunately I fear that it will continue to affect me in ways I haven't even imagined yet. There are things I do now that I don't understand. Sometimes I look in the mirror and I don't recognise the person staring back at me. Sometimes I repeat the same word over and over and over. Until I feel safe. Until I feel like I own that word. I'm afraid of the dark, I'm afraid of bathrooms, I lock myself in so quickly in any bathroom. I listen before I unlock, and when I do I race out so quickly. I'm afraid of alcohol, of strangers, of friends. I'm afraid of men I've known my whole life. I'm afraid of stairs, I don't really know why but I now race up and down them and try to never look back at them. I'm afraid of sleeping alone. My sister has gotten into my bed almost every single night. I am an 18 year old woman and I can't sleep without my little sister. I am embarrassed. And then I am ashamed that I am embarrassed. I am hard on myself for not being stronger and then I am mad at myself for being hard on myself. I am so scared, god I'm so scared, I spend so much of my time being scared. I have this knot in my chest that has become a permanent fixture, and I hate how afraid I am but I also hate how much I am afraid how people would judge me if I wasn't afraid. I'm afraid of the day that I'm not afraid because I really don't know what emotion could replace that. And that scares me so much.

But that is all just me. That doesn't even take into account all the other people in my life that this has affected. My parents, my sister, my whole family. All of your relationships shift, they all change when you tell people this. My little sister, she is the person I am supposed to protect. Yet as I said, she is the one helping me fall asleep every night. My mum and dad, clinical examiners, nurses were not supposed to talk to them about their daughters vagina" I squirmed inside as I said these words, despite the fact that I knew I was going to…I carried on. 'They were not supposed to have to take endless days off work to look after me. Yes, take care of me when I'm sick, when I have the flu, not look after me for something that never needed to happen. My friends, we're supposed to laugh about the boys we sleep with. Tell each other stories, advice, take care of each other. Love each other. I don't really know what it's like to see a friend go through this, so I can't speak for them but this was our last year in school together. We were not supposed to spend so much of it in silences, in bringing me home schoolwork, in protecting me in the hallways on the rare days I made it in, in not going out and staying in with me'

I took another deep breath, a lot of this was only pouring out of me as a spoke. I didn't realize how much I had thought of all these things subconsciously until I was saying them.

'This isn't all about me. This one night, this one act, this act of violence that he did to me didn't just end with me. It didn't stop when he was finished and walked away. It had a ripple effect. It has affected so many people connected to me, forever. So I'm not doing this just for me. But I do question daily if this is helping me or hurting me, as much as I want justice for myself and as much as I want justice for all the other girls and boys whose cases didn't make it. Who's never even made it this far because there are thousands of them. There are far too many. I'm not doing this to gain publicity or sympathy or whatever it is that you might think I would like to get out of this. I'm not getting anything out of this, trust me. I know now that if I had wanted to start my healing process straight away, I wouldn't have told anyone. Mending….if that's the right word for it, is not something that happens in front of everyone. It is not done well in front of an audience. In front of a literal judge. I know that now. Having to stand up here right now, for me anyways is not healing. But it is changing. It is the fighting part' I took a deep breath and paused. My hands were clenched. I couldn't look at anyone or I would fall apart. Twenty more seconds Scarlett. You can do this I told myself.

'When I decided to go through with this trial I knew it was the end of everything I was and knew. I knew there was no going back. I was right, there is no going back, there is no escape route from this, I will never be the person I was before. That girl, that woman is gone. She has become...I'm not even quite sure yet. But a lot of people seem to think they know me. It seems to be that because I have reported an assault that they should automatically be entitled to my whole history. They wanted to know everything about me....while all I wanted to know was how to make this better...' I choked on the last words. Kevin looked up at me, but I nodded reassuringly back at him.

'I'm not doing this all for me....' I tear rolled down my face 'I'm doing this because, I'm doing this because I know now that out of every 1000 sexual assaults, 995 of the perpetrators will walk away free. That there's a tiny amount of people that actually pay for the crime that they committed, and that's because in today's world, a woman's word is first doubted before it is believed and there is something so fundamentally wrong with that? I'm doing this in the hope that maybe I will bring up the statistics by even half of a percent, in the hope that one day others won't be afraid to speak up and say something. Say something, because if we don't' I took a breath 'if we don't thing's will never change. And as much as I love this world, some things need to change.'

I exhaled loudly, the court was completely silent. I felt I needed to say just a little bit more. There was more fight left in me now.

'If we don't speak.... then this becomes normal and this becomes common. And who wants to live in a world where something so awful is so accepted...

I'll finish now but...I just want to say that I am not just a few hours on the 31st of October. I am not what I wore and what I drank and who I spoke to and which direction I walked in the hall. That was a few hours of my 17 years on this planet. In reality it was mere minutes. I am more than that. I am a human being, not a number or an outlier or just another victim. I am Scarlett.'

One member of the Jury had a tear rolling down her face, we made eye contact and I quickly looked down. That was all I had to say, I was done. The hard things, we can do them.

Eva (female on the Jury)

"she said she forgave him because it meant she could walk into nightclubs and not freak out when she saw the back of a head that she thought looked like his"

We'd picked Marie as the foreman. Up until recently I didn't know what a foreman was. A jury picks one to speak on behalf of us I guess was her role. She seemed to think that meant she would lead all discussions because of this. I couldn't care less and she was the loudest out of us all anyways so maybe she picked herself more than we picked her.

I was really annoyed when I got asked to be on a jury and then when I heard about what the case was I got kind of excited because I guess I thought I'd see some stuff. But it was a way longer process than I thought to even end up on the actual jury of twelve of us who are here.

I didn't really know what I thought of the rest of them. We'd spent a lot of time together now at this stage but they were all so different to me. Usually when I was outside of my comfort zone, I could always figure out who was from my area or who would know someone I knew and I could go towards them and we'd find someone or something in common. I liked that about town, Dublin wasn't a big city. But in here everyone was dressed so similarly for court that at the start I couldn't tell where anyone was from

I liked Gemma, she cried a lot though, especially when we were given all the details. Gemma was a few years younger than me, she was studying archaeology which I thought was mad. Who the hell spends all that money to study old dead stuff. She was also in Trinity so I guessed it didn't matter what she wanted to study she obviously was going to be able to give everything a go. Gemma was worried that all this time spent here was going to affect her grades though. I told her not to sweat it that she could always repeat. Gemma then had a look on her face as though that was something she had never ever considered. She shook her head.

I was a bit worried too but not for the same reasons as Gemma, I was worried I would lose my job.

My manager really wasn't happy with me recently. I had to miss so many days for this trial, for that little girl. She really was so tiny. It had all seemed a bit silly to me at the start to be honest. When I first heard rape case I thought it was going to be brutal and involve a dark street and I don't know a paralysed girl or something. Maybe a kidnapping. Scarlett was perfect, she was gorgeous and it was so obvious she came from a real good family. We couldn't speak to her or anyone of course but sometimes when I saw her I was so tempted to just shout 'why are you doing this, he's not worth it' But of course I didn't. Marie wouldn't have liked that. She liked the rules. She was always asking the court for more info on what exactly they were saying. She would then be reading us out proper definitions of laws and what exactly that would mean for the accused. Brian would always speak out when she started at this. Brian was in his late 30's I guessed. He was kind of fit for that age though I thought.

'Marie we're not supposed to try and understand the law, we are here to deal with what evidence we have and to make the decisions based on what is in front of us' he said today as we sat in a circle and Marie read out yet another explanation of a law. I had zoned out which I knew I shouldn't but I also knew that usually what Marie said had no actual meaning.

'I was looking straight at her as she made that statement' said a woman called Judy, Judy was a mindfulness coach. I really wondered how one became one of those. 'I was looking at her and it was so raw, she was so there, it was all her. Every word that came out of her mouth was her own, I just know it'

'It made me cry' said the lady sitting next to her, I don't quite know what she did but she had about five kids and always brought us in cakes and bits that she'd baked.

Tom, an older man I his fifties, he didn't say much usually, sighed and turned to the whole group 'we need to be looking at what's in front of us. What do we do with what we have?' he was exasperated and wanted this all to end. I felt that. It's not like my life stacking shelves and asking young people for ID was what I was really missing but to be honest I didn't want to be thinking about Scarlett any more. I didn't like men much, I didn't really have any in my life to be honest. It was me, my mum and my sister who was never home because she always had a new man in her life. Which to me meant she always had someone new to cry about. She moved on quick though which made me think that half the things she said they did to her they didn't really do because would she really still trust men. I don't know, she always told me I knew nothing, that I was too young.

I didn't really believe that any more but I still heard her voice in my head when I was trying to do something that scared me. It was silly I knew that much but I also couldn't help but think she was older so maybe she did know better.

Gemma next to me gave me a nudge "what are you thinking?" I was suddenly brought back to the room. The circle. The decision we were all supposed to make. We were struggling. It was hard enough to be vocal in a group, let alone a group of people we didn't know a long time. I could barely voice my opinion with my friends that I had known since I could talk.

'Ehm, I don't know, what are you thinking? I asked right back. The rest of the group were all talking in little circles themselves now so we weren't alone in having our own discussion.

Gemma swallowed "I was talking to my friend last night...she, well she had a bad sort of incident a while ago with a guy. I know him, we all know him but ehm..." I nodded, encouraging her to go on. "Yes well I'm getting off track, what I'm trying to say is that she didn't feel good about the situation but in the last few months she's started to say that she forgives him" Gemma was looking at me, searching my face for a reaction. I'd learned that art of a poker face a long time ago, my mum's mood swings meant I spent a lot of time being on the receiving end of long, never-ending rants and rages and ups and downs. When I was young I figured out the easiest way to make them end most peacefully was to not react at all, it's hard to keep fighting with a blank wall. When I didn't react to Gemma she continue to speak "she said...Taylor's her name, my friend I mean, and she said she forgave him because it meant she was now free. I remember it so clearly Eva, she said she forgave him because it meant she could walk into nightclubs and not freak out when she saw the back of a head that she thought looked like his. Oh Eva she used to be so scared of going out. Of seeing him. She said she's forgiven him so that she doesn't have to live in that fear any longer." I nodded, to show her that I was listening "she said she forgave him so that she could finally forgive herself. She blames herself so much and forgiving him meant that it wasn't too bad, that she didn't have to blame herself for anything I think?'

'Hmm' I said, I was thinking that it made sense though. I do think if it happened to me I would just fully pretend that it didn't, that probably wouldn't be healthy but I didn't see the point in everything that say Scarlett was doing right now. What was this going to get her in the end. Even if she did win, would that work, would she then feel better?

'What would you decide Eva?' asked Gemma 'if it was only up to you, if it didn't have to be a group decision here. What would you do?'

I thought for a moment, and I thought of how I had no really good experience with any men at all. I didn't care about them.

'I would find him guilty' I said carefully, not knowing how Gemma was going to respond to what I was going to say 'but I wouldn't find him guilty for the right reasons. I'd find him guilty because all I've really seen men do is hurt the people I care about, and he just happens to be a man and for once in my life it feels like I have the power over the man. So yes I would find him guilty, but I can't say that I know for sure he is guilty, I don't think any of us can know. I think we should just believe her'

Gemma nodded 'I think you're right…it shouldn't be so complicated'

'How is your friend now?' I asked 'How is Taylor?'

'She's so good, she wasn't for a long time. I don't know if she's detached herself or if this whole forgiveness thing has really worked but she's honestly doing so well'

I smiled, 'I'm glad, I guess it's different for everyone…'

Maria stood up

'Tom's right' the whole group took in a breath, those were words we had never heard Maria say – that someone else was right. 'We need to be looking at what's right in front of us, not what could be or should be'

'I think we should take an anonymous vote' said Gemma 'everyone write down guilty or not guilty on a piece of paper, we don't have to use it as our decision but just to get an idea. It might make us think we really want the opposite of what comes up most strong'

I nodded, trying to show my support with that idea. Bless Gemma.

'I agree, let's just do it' said Brian, standing up and leaving the room. He returned with paper and pens.

We all were silent as we wrote and then Maria walked around and collected them all. I was tapping my foot against the floor as she separated the pieces of paper into two piles that were looking extremely equal in height.

'Here Brian will you double count these for me' asked Maria,

Brian kneeled down next to her in the middle of the circle. His lips were mouthing the numbers but I couldn't read them. He nodded and handed the piles back to Maria.

'Okay, this is what we have right now' said Maria and she told us what we had voted for. Gemma and I looked at each other. I gave her hand a squeeze.

We made our decision that day. Soon we would be sitting watching Scarlett hear that decision.

6

Awaiting Trial Results

Scarlett

"Because no, I wasn't wrong. Going outside late at night is not terrible. It is not something to fear, it is beautiful and cold and clear and sparkly'.

I couldn't help but think about all the terrible things that could have happened to me, but hadn't. When I was growing up my grandmother used to always say, if everyone put their problems into a pile in the middle of a circle and then everyone in the circle had to pick a problem to have, everybody would pick back up their own problems. Because we know them. Because as humans we can get used to almost anything. If we think about it too much it is terrible how quickly something shocking becomes a normal part of life.

But would I really pick this back up? I thought of all the brutal things that happen to people every single day; continuous abuse, emotional manipulation, murder, physical abuse, accidents that lead to a life in a wheelchair, accidents that lead to a life of never speaking or hearing or seeing. Accidents that lead to death.

None of these terrible things had happened to me. I had been given this awful thing, this assault, these memories, but for me, my awful thing was not the end. I thought about how the end could be tomorrow, it could be three years away or it could be over ninety. And if that end is either a day or ninety away from me, am I really going to survive this awful thing only to let it seep and manipulate its way into all the magic of the life I still have. The body, the mind, the people I still have. Was I going to let it turn all of that terrible too. Did I have the power to stop it. Maybe not. But could I try? I didn't know the answers. No one had taught me, no one could teach me is what I guessed.

Because no, I wasn't wrong. Going outside late at night is not terrible. It is not something to fear, it is beautiful and cold and clear and sparkly. Being in a nightclub or at a party surrounded by friends and strangers is not awful, it is exciting, and heartwarming and full of surprises. My body being the way it is, in whatever it is clothed in is not shameful, or revealing or promiscuous, it is an expression of myself. It is me feeling comfortable.

My body outside of clothes or lack of clothes is not an object of desire. It is allowing me to do every single thing I want to do, it is letting me climb and run and dance and hug and jump. Getting into a taxi is not dangerous, it is a way home. It is a shelter from rain and cold and it is music to hum to as you look at the photos you took that night. Going for a run after work with your headphones in is not stupid or careless, it is looking after your mind and your body and it is feeling the cold on your face and the ache in your muscles the next morning. Travelling alone is not a death wish, it can be daunting but it also can be life changing and challenging and the best adventure. Flirting with someone you just met is not reckless, unsafe or an open invitation for more. It is one of the most human interactions, it is new connections and forming stories for the future. It could very well be the start of a love story. Going home with a stranger is not idiotic, asking for it or absolutely terrifying. It is so human, it is faith in humanity and it is very often the beginning of a new chapter.

The thing is, it's only when bad things happen that we think of the danger of doing the said thing. It's only when something goes wrong that we reflect and think that, maybe she shouldn't have chatted up to that guy, she shouldn't have worn that, she shouldn't have gone there. However, the actual act of running or of getting into a taxi is not more dangerous for a female than it is for a male. We live in the same world. We can run just as safely as long as no one decides to follow us on our run. We are capable of going on a blind date just as safely as any male, just as long as our date decides to not do anything to harm us. It is only more provocative or 'asking for it' for a woman to not wear a shirt because of the reaction of the surrounding males. This world is more dangerous for females simply because of the things males could potentially do. That is all.

Another thing my grandmother had taught me was for when something hurt I would count down from ten until the pain died down. I would be concentrating on the counting so much and on the hope that the pain would end once I reached one that it used to make things like stubbing my toe of the side of the table or falling over in the back yard a lot easier. If something really hurt she would sometimes get me to pretend that I was holding an egg in one hand and to hop up and down on one leg pretending I was trying to balance the egg. I loved that one. I still do that this day. But I can't do that with this. Sometimes, mostly in the mornings when I'm chopping up fruit for my smoothie and trying to remind myself that I can do this day. That I will do this day. Sometimes I like to think of analogies, this morning as I cut up raspberries I was thinking of breaks and sprains. I was thinking about how this hadn't broken me but in the same way that it was difficult to explain how a sprain was sometimes worse than a break, it was difficult to explain how confused and conflicted I felt daily. I wasn't broken, but like a sprain, there would be a weakness there forever.

My mum came into the kitchen. 'Morning' she said as I put my raspberries into the blender. 'Morning, I'm not going in today again if that's okay' I said. I then pushed down the button on the blender so she couldn't answer me straight away. I knew I needed to be going to school, I knew I needed to face my fear, mostly I knew my mum was terrified of me getting trapped in this habit. But these days were intense, we were expecting a call anytime of any day to tell us that the jury had reached their verdict. I was dreading it but I also wanted the phone to ring so badly. This whole process had been horrible, no matter what I just wanted it to be over. I lifted my finger off the button on the blending machine. Silence. Mum sighed, 'it will be soon hon, it really will. But no matter what, please remember that life will carry on despite what they decide okay' I poured my smoothie into two glasses 'it's not up to them, you know and we know what happened. You've done all you can'

I handed her a glass. Samantha walked into the kitchen in her uniform, she noted my lack of one. 'Scarlett come on, you've got to go some-day'

I sipped my smoothie 'can that day not be today' I said bluntly, reverting to my dry humour as I had become far too accustomed to doing so recently.

'Today will be easy, the girls are all going to be there for you and I'll be there too. It will be okay he's not going to school'

I couldn't think about him so I shoved that 'him' down.

'That smoothies good Scarlett' my mum smiled softly 'look, this will end and this will pass. And when it does, you're going to want to be able to move on to amazing things, going to school can help those amazing things happen. There's only a few days left of school, you don't want to have missed the end'

I sighed and my dad walked into the kitchen. All dressed for work, it would be mum and me at home again. He clocked the situation, it was a morning routine he now knew well. In the beginning he had taken part, tried to convince me to go, agreed with mum and Samantha.

'Morning' he said and put on the kettle. He didn't try, I didn't want to be the person that people had given up on trying to convince. That wasn't me.

'Okay' I said, finishing my smoothie. 'I'm going but give me twenty minutes'

I raced up the stairs before anyone could even answer me. My uniform was laid out perfectly outside my door, courtesy of Samantha every single week day recently. I put it on, I had lost weight, I ran more, I ate less. I added another layer underneath and I looked more like me, one less thing for people to talk about. I went into the bathroom and put on BB cream. I opened my phone and text the groupchat, Liv, Bee and Maddy 'I'm coming in girls, can we meet at usual spot in 20?'

Within seconds I had three responses in the group and private message from each of them. Things might be heart-breaking and messy in my life right now but I had my people. I went back downstairs and Samantha had my bag in her hand. 'Come on, we're gonna be late'

Mum and dad walked us both to the door, like they had done years and years ago when we first started walking to school alone. Mum squeezed me tight, 'call me anytime please' I looked at her 'you too' my dad kissed my forehead.

Samantha closed the door behind us. Less than two hours later I would be back here. We got the call.

18 year old male acquitted of sexually assaulting young female.

May 12th 2019, 2:20PM 56,649 views 0 comments

A young Dublin man has been found not guilty of raping a woman he knew at a Halloween Party in 2017.

The now twenty year old male who cannot be named for legal reasons pleaded not guilty to an offense of rape against the woman at a private residence on the 31st October 2017. The man was eighteen at the time of the crime.

The complainant was seventeen at the time of the alleged crime. She, who will not be named due to legal reasons was in the same school as the young man. The young female says she was intoxicated at the time, was unable to consent and had attempted to stop him. The young female suffered injuries to her head and bruising to her body. The alleged crime took place in the bathroom of the female's friend's house. The next day she reported to the Garda.

The accused told the jury that he had previously had sexual relations with the woman and she gave no indicator that she was not interested on this occasion. He stated that all sexual activity was consensual and any injuries were as a result of consensual sexual activity. His lawyers submitted that it was a busy party and no noises were heard from the bathroom.

Today, the jury of six men and six women came back with a verdict of not guilty. The accused was then discharged and walked free from the court.

In the woman's victim impact statement, which was read out by the woman before the court, the young woman spoke of how she is now 'afraid of men she's 'known her whole life' She spoke of all the people that this one moment in her life has now impacted, that this was not just a crime against her but an incident that has affected many people around her.

In closing for the defense, the young man's defense said that it was too unclear for the young man to have known he was sexually assaulting her if she had not clearly stated this. It was also emphasised that the young woman had been involved in sexual relations with the accused before. It was said that there were inconsistencies in the young woman's account as she was unclear as to how she ended up in the bathroom. They named her to be unreliable.

Comments are closed for legal reasons.

Helpline: Dublin Rape Crisis Centre: 1800 778 888

7

2 years later

22 year old male sentenced for raping young woman.

March 16th 2021, 5.52PM

83 973 views 0 comments

A man has been sentenced to six years following sexually assaulting a twenty one year old female at a private residence in South Dublin last September.

The twenty two year old male who cannot be named for legal reasons pleaded not guilty to an account of rape of the women at his Dublin home in the early hours of September 18th. The same man was involved in a similar case in the Central Criminal Court two years prior to this.

The twenty two year old man expressed no outward emotions this morning as a majority verdict of guilty was returned by the jury following a trial in the Central Criminal Court.

The female had gone home with the male following a night out in town with a large group of friends. They were said to have known each other vaguely through college friends. She said there was absolutely no consent and that she was highly intoxicated at the time of the crime. She left his home around 3am in distress The female had sustained a wound to her head, marks on her hands and marks on her neck.

The defendant says the sex was completely consensual and was initiated by the female. He said she left quickly and he did not know why. He himself said he was intoxicated and in relation to any injuries sustained he reported they were all as a result of sexual activity that was asked for by the female.

The man was sentenced to a six years imprisonment but the last twenty-four months were suspended on the strict conditions that the man be of good behaviour for six years post release. It was also ordered that the man have no contact whatsoever with the victim.

The case was said to have been aggravated by the accompanying violence, and the severe impact on the victim.

It was said that the mitigating factors in this case were the perpetrators age as he was just twenty one at the time of the crime and the fact that he had no prior convictions.

Comments are closed for legal reasons.

Helpline: Dublin Rape Crisis Centre: 1800 778 888

8

October 31st
WHAT REALLY HAPPENED

*J*oel shut the bedroom door softly behind him, following a stumbling but beautiful Scarlett over to a large double bed.

'I can't, I can't believe you're here' she laughed loudly, sprawling herself backwards onto the white and pink duvet. Joel sat down on the edge of the bed.

'It's been a while alright' he said, then turned to her 'but listen Scarlett' he took her hand and pulled her gently up from lying down so that she was sitting next to him.

'I'm sorry...I really am... I'm so sorry. I was really young and ...'

Scarlett moved her face inches from Joel's

'shh' she whispered placing her finger over his lips.

Joel took her hand away and kissed her. She swayed from side to side unintentionally and started giggling mid-way. Joel realized how drunk she was. How he had never seen her this drunk. He placed his hand on her bare thigh, pushing her skirt slightly up higher.

'So long' she said, suddenly serious. 'it's been so long" she paused and smiled "I cried Joel' she laughed, loudly 'I really cried' suddenly her face contorted, and she put a hand over her mouth.

'I might get sick' she looked sick, thought Joel. His mind raced, she was so hot he thought. Why had he screwed up what they had? Couldn't he just kiss her until she was better, he leaned in towards her once more and she kissed him back, she let his hand go under her red velvet top. Joel pulled his face away, leaving his hand where it was.

'Can we make this work Scarlett? Could you forgive me?' he asked suddenly feeling serious.

'In a heartbeat' smiled Scarlett. Joel smiled back and leaned over to lie down on top of her, but she rolled over to her side and retched over the side of the bed. Joel sat up, a slight annoyance in his tone as he asked

'Are you alright?'

'I... I'm fine I just' she retched again before giggling and shaking her finger at herself 'Bad Scarlett, the one-time hahahah'

She lay back and shut her eyes. 'I sleep' she said softly lifting her hand up to touch Joel's knee softly.

'Wait Scarlett no' Joel shook her shoulders 'Look I'll get you some water, come on Scarlett I've waited so long for this'

She fluttered her eyes open...'Water' she nodded and licked her plump red lips. She curled up onto her side.

'Stay here I'll be right back, Scarlett' he looked back at her lying on the bed in her sexy devil's costume. One horn fallen off. He knew he only had the courage to say this because she was half asleep.

'Uh huh' she replied raising one foot limply as some form of response.

'Scarlett.... I really loved you and honestly' Joel sighed "I think I still do' her eyes were closed, she didn't reply.

'Take a nap, I'll be back with some water' Joel closed the door gently behind him.

Ten minutes later Scarlett opened her eyes, had Joel been here she thought, or had she imagined that whole scenario. No, he had been here, he had told her he loved her. She smiled with happiness, disbelief and in her drunken state she sighed out loud; after all this time Joel had never stopped loving her. Scarlett went to sit up, the whole dark room spun, and she remembered how drunk she was. She cursed herself for ruining the night. The one night. After stumbling off the bed, Scarlett made it to the door. She needed to apologize to Joel right, yes, for what? She forgot why Joel had been here, how she had ended up with him exactly but she knew he loved her and right now that seemed to be all that mattered.

She opened the door and the light from the hallway hurt her eyes. There was a loud thumping, techno music, thought Scarlett. She stepped outside and almost fell over a boy, 'Scarlett' he yelled loudly. He was drunk too thought Scarlett. She didn't reply, she couldn't remember his name and she felt too bad to ask. All of a sudden, she felt overwhelmingly sick and she puked onto the floor; narrowly missing the boy who had called her name. He didn't even notice, he started singing a song. Scarlett sank to the ground, her conscience drifting she closed her eyes.

'And I will always loveeee youu' yelled the guy on the floor jolting Scarlett awake again. Love, she thought, didn't Joel love her. She had to find him, tell him she loved him too. Tell him she had never stopped loving him, that she'd had no choice. She got herself up off the floor, her skirt ridding up her back she attempted to pull it down and grabbed the stair banister. She lost her step in her heels and fell down two steps before regaining her balance.

'Stupid shoes' Scarlett muttered, sitting down on the steps and taking them off, she left them on the steps and continued down barefoot. The music was loud in the hallway and the place was full of nameless faces that Scarlett couldn't distinguish between. She walked towards the living room and suddenly saw a mop of brown hair.

'Joel' she shouted out loudly, people turned to look at her, looking her up and down before returning to their conversations. Without having her crew of girls around her it wasn't as easy to not feel self-conscious from their stares. It wasn't as easy to shake it off. She stumbled towards the mop of hair and placed her hands drunkenly around his waist.

'Hey there' he spun around from who he was talking to.

'David? What…' Scarlett pulled away, but he kept her hands firmly around his waist by subtly holding them there.

'Scarlett there you are' Scarlett looked up, David was talking to Maddy and there she stood in her angel outfit, red cup in hand. She raised her eyes at Scarlett. The room started to spin again for Scarlett and David gripped her even tighter

'Whoa there Scarlett, are you okay?' asked David. Scarlett could feel Maddy's eyes boring into hers, Scarlett felt like she was forgetting something. Was Maddy okay? Why wouldn't David let her go.

'I need to find Joel' she said quietly, Maddy squinted at her 'What did you say? Scarlett are you okay?'

'Need to… I want to find Joel' said Scarlett again, louder this time and David heard.

'What did she say?' shouted Maddy over the music.

'She needs to go, she wants me to go with her' said David. Scarlett was turned around looking for Joel and was not keeping track of the conversation; David was still keeping her hands gripped under his on his waist. She tried to break free, starting pulling her hands away.

'I'd better go with her' shrugged David.

Maddy rolled her eyes 'have fun Scarlett....' Then quieter she sighed as she turned and walked away. Scarlett hadn't heard her. When she turned around Maddy was gone.

'Come on, I'll get you where you need to go' said David pulling Scarlett out of the room with him. The hallway had emptied, everyone was running out the front door because someone had shouted fireworks. It was, after all, Halloween night. Scarlett remember suddenly.

'Oh no' said Scarlett putting her hand over her mouth. She was going to get sick. She made a mental note to never drink wine again.

'Quick, bathroom' said David, opening the door to the bathroom under the stairs and quickly pulling Scarlett in after him. She leaned over the sink, in the mirror her face was pale, her mascara running and her dark red lipstick only leaving a stain on her lips. She looked a mess.

'I just...I lie.... I need to lie down' she stuttered, stepping away from the sink and sinking onto the floor beside the bath tub. David sat down next to her.

'You sleep, I'll look after you' he said

Scarlett nodded in response, she didn't have to energy to ask why he was there and not Maddy, her eyes were pulling themselves together and she drifted off.

...

Glass of water in hand, Joel started to head back toward the stairs. Scarlett would drink this, sober up and then they could talk and well hopefully do more than talk, but all in good time he thought and grinned to himself.

'You're looking happy cousin' smiled Liv bumping into him at the bottom of the stairs.

'Hey Liv, great party' said Joel brightly.

'Thanks Joel, you're having a good time so?'

'A great time, Liv' he paused, considering whether or not telling Liv would be a good idea right now. Would she warn Scarlett against him again? He couldn't help himself, he felt he had to share his news with someone, and Scarlett had always done what she wanted to anyways, not what others wanted her to. He knew she valued Liv's opinion but also knew Scarlett was one of the few people he knew that wasn't influenced by her best friends opinions. So he went for it.

"I think me, and Scarlett have patched things up'

Liv's face dropped 'Joel' she started, the tone of her voice a warning sign that she was about to launch into a lecture. But he was expecting this.

'Liv, I've changed. I promise, I won't hurt her again; I'm not an idiot. Look I'm even bringing her this water' he lifted up the glass.

Liv looked confused 'Why?'

'I think she had a bit too much to drink, she just needed a rest and some water and then we can talk'

'Scarlett had too much to drink, where is she? I need to check on her, she doesn't do that kind of stuff' Liv looked around anxiously.

'No Liv, listen, calm, I'll look after her I promise' Joel raised his pinkie finger 'I know she's your best friend I'll be a good boy'

Liv looked reluctant but raised her pinkie finger. 'Fine but if she gets worse just come and get me, I'll be outside with Mitch' she blushed. Liv would have the worst poker face.

Joel winked 'have fun cousin'

Liv rolled her eyes and walked away. Joel made his way up the stairs. The door to the bedroom was still closed but now there was some guy passed out outside of it. Joel stepped over him carelessly, hitting his foot and waking him up. He ignored him and went to open the door, it wasn't fully closed he realized, hadn't he closed it after him. 'Scarlett' he called, walking into the dark room. He flicked on the lights, she wasn't there. Where the fuck was she? He walked back outside,

'Hey dude did a girl come out of there?' he asked the semi-conscience guy.

All he got in response was a grunt. Joel checked the upstairs bathroom and opened another unlocked bedroom door.

'Whoa sorry guys, that's not Scarlett is it?"

'What the fuck get out' yelled some guy, a girl yelled back 'I'm not a Scarlett, please shut the door' Joel made out a girl with brown hair in the bed next to the guy. No not Scarlett. Thank god. 'Sorry' he yelled closing the door.

He started going down the stairs when he noticed something he had missed on his way up, shoes, Scarlett's shoes; he had only known they were hers because they had two little devil horns on the side of each. He picked them up, where had she gone he thought.

He continued down the stairs, shouting her name in the hallway, now crowded with people all talking about some fireworks they had just seen. The front door was open and the cold wind from outside was blowing he. He shivered as he squeezed his way through the crowd and into the kitchen, where he noticed just how many more people had arrived. The place was packed. He spotted Maddy sitting on the couch, she would know where Scarlett was. He raced over to her, shoes still in hand to find her sitting comforting a crying Liv.

'Shit Liv, are you okay?' he asked

She shook her head 'I...I'm fine'

Maddy gave him a look as if to say don't ask anymore, 'Mitch' she mouthed to him over Liv's head. Maddy looked pissed off, thought Joel, maybe she didn't want to be looking after her crying friend on Halloween night.

'Well have you guys seen Scarlett?' Maddy looked down and continued to stroke Liv's hair 'I can't find her anywhere' continued Joel.

'She went off with David' said Maddy simply.

'David? David who? Who the fuck is David?' asked Joel. Liv looked up at Joel sadly.

'Joel, Scarlett....' She looked to Maddy

'Basically, Scarlett can get off with anyone and everyone whenever she wants, and tonight it seems like she decided to go for the guy I liked' Maddy rolled her eyes but there were tears behind her sarcasm 'she can literally get fucking anyone, why did she need to do this' she said.

Liv pulled her head onto her shoulder, 'shhh Maddy it'll be okay, she shouldn't have done that. It's not fair'

'Yeah, I love her I do. I never thought she would do something like this..' Maddy looked up at Joel, he was standing in shock. Pale. Scarlett was getting with someone else was all he could think.

'What do you mean she can get off with everyone?" he asked Maddy and Liv, speaking slowly.

Neither of them replied. Joel's stomach dropped. He realized just how much he didn't like to think about her with other people.

Stupid Scarlett, he thought, just when I told her I loved her. He shook his head and thought I'm never talking to her again. Also, he needed to ask himself why this bothered him so much when he hadn't exactly been the picture of kindness to her. But that was too difficult to think about. It was much easier to dislike her. And even easier to dislike her for her ability to do what she wanted.

'Liv, this was a great party but I think I might head home okay'

Liv nodded, red eyed. 'Happy Halloween' said Maddy feebly, shutting her eyes and resting herself on Liv.

Joel smiled weakly. 'Where's the bathroom actually? I know I've been here before but just point me in the right direction…this place is packed' his mind was whirling and he couldn't think straight. He should have never let Scarlet go.

'Under the stairs' said Liv pointing towards the hallway. Joel nodded 'See you guys' he placed the un-drank glass of water on the counter in the hall and tried to open the bathroom door. He knocked, girls at parties always spent far too long nattering in toilets he thought when there are people who actually needed to go and pee.

'Hurry up' he knocked loudly 'I'm dying out here' There was no response. It was strangely quite in there. No giggles or chatter.

He knocked again, louder this time and tried to turn the handle. 'Dude go away' shouted a boy's voice from inside.

'Hey can I just use the bathroom' shouted Joel. Silence. He kept knocking.

'No, go away, I mean it. Fuck off' shouted the voice back. Joel gave up. 'Prick' he shouted in at him, knocking loudly one more time just to piss him off. Joel zipped up his jacket and walked out the front door. He took his phone out of his pocket and ordered a Free Now and told himself that he wouldn't think about Scarlett any more.

Scarlett woke up to a bang. Noise, knocking. She tried to sit up but the room was spinning. Had she blacked out, where was she again. Her stomach turned and her head ached.

"Hey there" said a voice, Scarlett looked up, sitting opposite her with his back against the door was a boy, but there was no lights on. Scarlett's head hurt, she placed it between her legs. Everything was spinning again. "Ow" she let out a little moan referring to her pounding head.

'Hey shh' the boy crawled over to her. His face was moving blurry but Scarlett then knew who he was.

"David" she said, lifting her head up more "can....can you get my friends, I don't feel well please" Scarlett's body swung to her side and she rested herself down on the cold hard tiles. The corner of the bathroom mat under her head.

'Don't worry, I'll look after you" said David, pulling her gently onto his lap.

Scarlett started to protest "no, my friends please…please" her body was weak and she couldn't remember why she was in her, with him? Her heavy eyelids closed. She could feel her drunkenness, she could feel the weight of it in her mind and body. A moment or two later she opened her eyes again. A heavy weight against her.

'David' she spat out weakly, he was moving on top of her. His hand running up and down the inside of her leg. Scarlett flailed hopelessly against him.

'Come on Scarlett, we never got around to it… I know you're an expert…' he started to kiss her neck and up to her face. Scarlett pushed at his strong shoulders, fear was waking her up. Her tiny weak body was a dead weight under his, he pushed up her skirt. She jolted and scratched his face, her long sharp fake nails drawing blood from just above his eyebrow. David pulled back

'Playing dirty are we…' he took her two hands and pinned them above her head using only one of his hands, with the other he pulled down her black lace underwear and unbuttoned himself.

'Stop.. stop..' her words were slow. Muddy and far between each other. She wasn't even sure they were coming out the way she wanted them to. Were loud enough. David was moving himself closer. Scarlett wanted to scream, she wanted her body to be stronger. She willed herself against the alcohol and gave one last kick with one leg.

David's face twisted as she made contact, 'you little bitch, what's wrong with me huh…' he was angry, aggressive, he shoved himself into her suddenly and hard and her head came up from the tiles and bounced back down. With a tiny thump everything went black for Scarlett.

• • •

When Scarlett came around a heavy, strong David was heaving in and out of her. She couldn't move. The pain was excruciating. She opened her mouth to scream but a only feeble cry came out. David covered her mouth with his sweaty hand. He kept going. He didn't stop. Scarlett drifted in and out of consciousness, her head pounding. In that bathroom time was nothing. It was an instant, it was five minutes, it was forever.

David was gone. Scarlett tried to sit up, her head thumped. She held on to the side of the bath and saw her underwear sitting on the edge. She slowly put them back on, still sitting down. She had no shoes on. Scarlett could hear Dua Lipa pounding through the speakers on the other side of the door. She held on to the edge of the sink to help her self up. Scarlett was afraid of the other side of the door, but she was more afraid of staying in this bathroom. She opened the door, surprisingly no one was in the hallway. Scarlett didn't want to speak to anyone, she made her way up the stairs as quickly as her legs would take her, they were shaking. She stumbled straight into Liv's room, turned on the lights to make sure no one else was in there. Her eyes were watering as she lay down on Liv's bed. She let out a sob, but that was it. No tears came.

Epilogue

Scarlett

I'm twenty six years old. Today I will graduate from university with my post grad degree in Law. I ended up going to Galway to study. A trial isn't like what they show in the movies and the tv shows, a single scene where everything seems to be decided by twelve people in the space of twenty seconds. A trial is even so different from the way I've tried to tell it in my story. There are no words that describe this out of body experience that somehow becomes your world. And it's not until you've spent a few days not looking over your case every second of every day because one wrong word and you're back to square one, not even back to square one, you're automatically an unreliable witness to your own body. There's no words for the days you spend wanting to give up, wishing you had never ever said a single word because where the hell is this going to get me. There are no words for the friends you will lose, the conversations you never ever thought you would have to have with family. There's no words to describe the feeling you get in your stomach when you know people are looking at you differently, when going into school feels next to impossible. There are no words to describe the months I lost, the life I would have been living had I not been hibernating in fear of doing a single thing wrong that would affect my trial.

There's no one way to tell that story. A trial takes over your whole life. A trial takes months, years. You need to be available, you need to be nearby. You need to be good and right and good and right and good and right over and over and again and again and again. You need to be composed and well dressed and look well, over and over and over. It's relentless.

I didn't stay in Dublin. I couldn't. I went away, I went to college in Galway. Dublin will always be my home, but after moving to Galway I soon found that Galway became my safe space. It wasn't an escape, Ireland is a small country and word travels very quickly but I had accepted that I would never escape no matter where I went because I would always be with me. I didn't need to escape. I just needed to build a home that didn't revolve around a few hours of my life on the 31st of October. I found that there. I found the sea, I found friends and these amazing people called housemates and parties and coffee shops and I found hours of the day that would pass without my assault being mentioned. That was the best thing I could ever dream of finding.

I loved Law, I was never bored. I put it down on my CAO when I was in an angry state of mind, I never dreamed that I would get it. I didn't know what I wanted but my dad was right. I can hold a good argument. My mum was also right, I've got heaps upon heaps of emotion. I'm spending next year in Honduras working with underprivileged kid. I don't know if I will be able for it, if I am good enough of a person to be even attempting this but I know I will try.

. . .

I lost my case. Is it terrible that I wasn't surprised. Maybe I had never thought that I would actually win the case, maybe I just needed to keep moving, keep doing. I broke down, of course. I almost didn't sit my Leaving Cert. I scraped by in my exams. I was really low. I felt so many things, I called myself so many names, stupid, idiotic, naïve, dramatic, but what got me through was that I had a future waiting for me if I could just push through that summer, I could build a new home, a new family and my case result shouldn't have the power to destroy all that. Hadn't I already gone through the worse by simply putting myself through that trial in the first place. Of course it's a lot easier to say this all now when I hold the knowledge that he is now in prison. Not for assaulting me but for doing the exact same thing to another woman. I hate that he had the access to do this again, I hate that another woman had to experience what I did for him to finally receive punishment, I hate that my case wasn't good enough but I also know that thanks to my case and thanks to the fact that his history was there, the second case was a lot more straight forward. It made me feel that I had made the right decision. However life as the girl who has accused a man of rape and lost her case is not easy. I received a lot of hate, I stayed away from home for a long, long time after moving to Galway. I was so afraid of seeing his friends, of seeing people from my old school. I stayed sheltered in my Galway bubble until the other young woman reached out to me. Asking for my help, for my advice. This gave me a new drive, this pulled me out of my hole. I do not like that she had to experience this for me to be pulled back up but I would be lying if I said the fact that she wanted to go to court too didn't help me feel better about my past decisions. She won, she was an amazing kind human who will always say 'we' won. Who will always say that thanks to me she was able to win.

• • •

Compassion. This is what my mum says has got me through the last few years. Compassion for the people around me, the capability to forgive. For myself mainly. When I was seventeen, on that Halloween night, I was so young and vulnerable and naïve. And although none of those things have anything to do with what happened to me, what happened to me forced me to grow up a lot sooner than I would have liked. But that didn't have to be all bad. Because in the last few years my life there has been a whirlwind of ups' and downs, of highs and lows. Good days and bad days. Of little wins and big losses. But the main thing, the most important thing is that on every single one of those days I was happy. Under whatever emotions the certain day or event brought, underneath all of that, my general state was of happiness. I am so lucky I felt this way. I know this may not be the case for many but I was lucky to be born with a mind that leaned towards happiness. I was born with a mind that helped me every single day.

A few months after my case had closed I was watching tv and the news came on, there was a case in which a thirty three year old mother of two was raped by a stranger on the streets and she died the next day in hospital. It hit me. It hit me really hard. Because I didn't think about how I was in a way, one of the survivors and not just in a physical sense. I am still here. I'm alive. I didn't die that Halloween night. Yes maybe for a long while a massive part of me felt violated and destroyed. A massive part of me does still feel that way and I don't know if that will ever go away. But in the end, I was one of the victims that survived. I didn't die. Another part to all of this that I didn't think of at the time was that for me, being assaulted didn't make me want to curl up into a ball and never ever have faith in the world again. Of course, there were moments that I did, I curled up, I cried, I broke down. But the simple fact that I was born into support, into love and I was also born with this inherent urge to always get back up, to keep fighting. Because of these supports I am who I am today.

And after years of meeting people in similar situations I know that our responses to assault can range from the depths of depression to a only going forward attitude. They can range from that in one single day. There are so many women walking around today without anyone knowing they have been assaulted. Their lives are being impacted but often no one knows. All reactions are valid, all reactions are justified. No reaction is wrong. No matter what, it is never ever the victims fault. I have learned that. I knew that in theory but now I know exactly what that means. It means I had to stop questioning my every move, my every choice, every outfit, every drink, every friend, every song, every picture, every video, every moment. Because the only moment that could have mattered was if I had asked the boy who assaulted me to have sex with me. And I didn't.

It is not my fault. I tell that to myself every single morning in the mirror, as I brush my teeth, as I brush my hair, as I clean my face. Repeat, repeat, repeat. And it's slowly sinking in. It's not a full belief yet. But the days I used to spend analysing my every movement on that that night have been reduced to hours and one day I hope that the hours I still spend analysing will become minutes. One day.

So there are days when I feel my privilege. My home, my family, the country I was born in. my access to services. But I do also know how unlucky I was, I'm not belittling what happened to me or anyone else in a similar situation. This didn't need to happen. However, for me, knowing how bad things could have gone was one of the main things that helped. It helped me to think of how I was alive. It helped me to think of how I survived this. And watching the news and realizing how many women are killed through sexual violence every single day made me realize how close to walking into another version of my life I was.

However I am most definitely not saying we should feel lucky for not dying due to a man's feeling of entitlement to a woman's body, we should not feel lucky for being the victim of pure aggression but surviving that aggression. We do not need to be grateful that we survived something that should never have happened in the first place. We do not need to feel obliged to find the light in the darkest places but for me it was my way forward. We do not need to say 'well it could be worse' Because yes, , that is a fact, things could always be worse. But couldn't the reverse be true too? Couldn't we strive towards a better?

Just because there are more than forty million victims of human trafficking globally, that's forty million people. People like you or me, predominately women who are being sold for mainly sex without their consent day after day. I don't think that can even sink into my brain properly.

Being sold for sex is their life. But just because this underbelly of the world exists does not mean sexual assaults like my case are not also a major problem. We can care and fight for both. One does not cancel the other, one worse does not make the other 'okay'. We don't need to feel pressured to say 'there are people being subjected to physical and sexual assault every day, we can't complain about a drunk encounter' Neither of these extremes should be happening in the world so of course we can care about them all.

Once I got some distance between myself and my case I was drove to be more passionate about life. I started to love more because there was no point in putting up barriers when after everything I had gone through, I realized people are who we need the most. I decided to be more open to opportunities and different people, all experiences. It didn't do this straight away but with time, therapy, lots of workshops and so much help, my heart had let in so many more people, my eyes had read support from hundreds of strangers, and although my ears had heard the worst things said about me, my brain wanted to listen to the goodness, the kindness of the right words. I opened up.

I opened up because I realized that, in one instant your life could be gone or irreversibly changed. Forever. And you don't have any control over when or how that could happen. In saying that, it doesn't go away. It never ever goes away. There is not a day that passes where I don't think of what happened to me. There is not a day that it doesn't cross my mind and make me wish it had never happened to me.

Because despite it contributing towards shaping me into the person I am today, it is not a choice I would have made, for this to be something that shaped me but it would be wrong of me to say it didn't because absolutely everything we do an encounter and meet shapes us. We are a compilation of our experiences, of the people we love and of the emotions we have felt. Despite all this though, we don't need bad things to happen to us in order for us to become good people. I am not compassionate, or more loving because I was sexually assaulted. No. I did not need that bad thing to happen to me for me to realize who I want to be in this world. I am the way I am because I made the decision to build myself into that person despite the obstacles that had been placed in my way. And I will say that as much as I am proud of young Scarlett and how much she accomplished by being tough and resilient and through being a powerful force. She was not the real me. She was not the me before the trial or the me after the trial. But sometimes the person you become in order to survive is not the person you necessarily want to be or is not your best self.

But from now on, I can only take control of the rest of my life. I can only try my very best every damn day to take it (the bad memories, the flashbacks, the fear of everything) in my hands and to throw them to the side. And I'll tell you this, far too many minutes of my one and only life are spent attempting to throw what happened to me to the damn side. And I won't lie, somedays it really does feel like a battle I don't win. It takes over and I feel afraid. More than afraid. Terrified. I feel afraid of life. But that's the thing, it's only the one life I have. I only have this version to experience. That parallel life, I can't touch her. I don't know how she is. Maybe I don't want to know. This is all I know. This is what I've got. I cannot go back, I can only ever move forward, only move towards a world where this happens less. To a world that only we, me and you, can try and make better and brighter and, as my mum would say, more compassionate.

'And, like all the best quests, in the end, I did it all for a girl: me'
Caitlin Moran

The End.

PART II

'Your Word'

The following stories are all true, anonymous accounts of sexual harassment and assault.

I did not expect to get such an overwhelmingly, interactive response from people when I decided to start asking others if they had stories they wanted to anonymously share.

I feel privileged to have been trusted with these stories and I am so grateful to each and every person who shared with me and with the world through this book.

Thanks to all of you, I hope 'Her Word' will have a much bigger impact than it did before it included all of your stories.

Through asking people for their own experiences of sexual assault or harassment I ended up as a side effect, gathering research. I asked 65 people if they had any experiences and out of this 29 people shared an experience or multiple experiences with me. This means, from the limited amount of people I asked, that 45% of these have an experience of sexual harassment or assault.

I have added in my own research to the end of some of the true pieces and I wrote them as objectively as I could. They are simply information I found.

Receiving and writing up these pieces was eye-opening, shocking and of course at times, heartbreaking but I think it is so important for it to be known that these are real people, real stories, real lives that are affected daily. These are the men and women we pass every day, therefore the perpetrators in these stories are also the people we pass every day. The issue is all around us and therefore is most definitely not one we can ignore.

Thank you all for being so brave and incredible.

Female, 21

As I sit here writing this, I'm in a space of two minds. My mind is telling me no - that I am looking for attention. That nobody wants to hear my pity story. My heart, still broken and bruised is screaming to let it all out.

Two and a half years. Two and a half years I called him the love of my life. My soulmate. The person who held my hand. Who pointed out the window when we drove and told me someday we would have a house like that one, or a car like that. Someday we would be each-others for better or for worse.

It all began when I moved to college. The guilt trips. The disgusting texts and messages I got. I had gotten my dream course in my dream college. I was attending the same University as some of the most powerful women and men that this country has seen, let it be from a political view or an artistic, a medical and scientific. I was there. And if felt so damn good.

The night before taking that big leap of faith and road-tripping, my family organized a small get together. My mum and dad were proud but heartbroken, their first to leave the pond.

But him – he was having nothing. He wanted the simple life – the settle down and get married and have babies sort of life. I never wanted that. I wanted more, so much more.

And with that he forced himself on me that night. I couldn't scream for help for fear my younger sister would hear. The tears streamed down my face. He knew what he was doing. It was the beginning that marked it all.

I became a shell in first year. I lost interest in everything I did. I turned to myself for comfort and shelter. I never left my room.

Depression swallowed me and became my bubble. I couldn't leave – nights out were non-existent. I remember one night going to Coppers with some of my beautiful, fantastic housemates, so excited to actually have a night out in college. Then it came through - *beep*- message after message after missed call after message; "Where are you?", "Probably at some lad's house", "You're going to fucking regret that". It swarmed me. I couldn't escape. That same night we couldn't get in because one of the girls were underage and I flipped. Not because of her, but because I was so afraid and could tell nobody.

Three months later, my phone went one night sitting in my room. Four random girls messaging me on Instagram. Another adding my snapchat. Looking through the messages, my heart sunk. The weight I had put on from depression binge eating became more noticeable when I grabbed my stomach. It wasn't a pouch anymore. It was twenty pounds of solid denial. There they were. His tinder profile. The nudes he had sent girls. The little video he had managed to record on a night out with a girl who wasn't even legal yet. The messages. Everything. It was all evident right in the palm of my hand.

The spiral went on for a few more months. "But I love you", "You're my future", "I might as well just commit suicide now then". The washing-machine guilt-trip affect. I had enough when he came to visit one night and I went to say goodnight to my dad. Afterwards when he was lying in bed next to me, he just gently whispers; "You know he could die any minute".

That was it. That was what I needed to hear to understand why he was who he had become. A monster. That was the last time he would ever step foot in my family's home or for that matter, my life ever again.

. . .

Shortly after, my relationship with myself began to build, but my respect for myself deteriorated. I began to question my ability to even look at men. I became an avid purchaser of the morning after pill. I enjoyed being mistreated and mentally abused. Because I knew no different. I never felt love. That was the problem. I even began to question my sexuality thinking that gender similarity had parallels in the feelings and emotions towards men. But I knew I was not attracted to women.

I took time. I thought. I built myself. I understood what I needed. I manifested.

Today, I am a better person. Mentally. Physically. I enjoy the littlest things in life. Good coffee, oat milk. Morning swims. Sunflowers. A good read. Beautiful artwork, Morning jazz and dancing in my kitchen whilst I make porridge. I've learnt to push myself. Physically. Mentally. I'm fitter, stronger. Academically, I'm empowering myself.

Regarding my relationships, a bit like my life in general – I don't know where this wonderful journey I'm currently on will bring and where my next destination is. There are somethings I know though for sure;

- Positive people are attracted by positive energy. Be the person you want to meet. Don't ever try to fall in love, it's a gift and a rare one. Let it happen as sporadically as it may come and go.

- Go out and enjoy every chance you get; life goes by in the blink of an eye. One day you may fall asleep, and your spirit may never return to the same body that lay down. Make memories.

- Always say sorry. Forgive and move on. Alas, don't hold guilt to anybody, it feeds off your happiness like a gauge.

- Give hugs and smile. You have teeth for a reason

- Use your sense and go with your gut – smell the coffee and the roses, listen to the birds and the waves and the music, read and watch those pieces, enjoy the taste of everything you nurture your body with (particularly the pints!) , and last but not least – if your gut is saying no, it means no!

Female, 21

The night he assaulted me I had given him a birthday card saying how happy I was to be his girlfriend and how lucky I was to have him. We were having sex upstairs during a party when he asked me if he could do something we had never done before. I said no but he did it anyway.

I have never felt so betrayed by anyone and it felt like I had done something wrong. I left straight away and rang my friend. She came with me to report what had happened. He gaslighted me, denying everything and called me out for insulting him before I left.

The next week I went away on a trip with my best friends and I never could have imagined how good I would feel with my closest friends by my side, they support me so much and it really helped me to heal.

We are so often told to stay away from the strange older men, the odd looking, the addicts, the homeless. The strangers. What we are not taught is that most abuse, most assaults are perpetrated by people we know. People we know so well.

1 in 4 women in Ireland have been abused by a current or former partner. It's not always the strangers on the streets. In fact, it rarely is.

And it's not just the fact that it happens; it's also how accepted it has become in society. 33% of women in Ireland perceived the frequency of violence against women to be 'very common'

Emotional and psychological abuse is very real but is often unseen or intangible to people outside of the relationship. It leads to outbursts or behavior that no one else can understand and that the victim feels like they cannot explain. It isolates people and this is exactly what the perpetrator wants. For the victim to feel alone, for them to feel as though they then only have them. For them to be even more afraid to leave.

Examples of emotional abuse include, being put down, being constantly criticized, threats to kill or harm, being monitored via phone or email.

Emotional abuse often occurs with physical or sexual abuse. In relation to sexual abuse, the most powerful thing I've learned is that the victim's home is the single most common location for incidents of rape to occur.

Less than 25% of people severely abused in relationships reported it to the guards.

It has been found that the effects of emotional abuse can be just as detrimental as the effects of physical or sexual abuse, yet the law does not recognize emotional abuse as a crime.

The effects of abuse are ongoing, they do not end when the abuse ends. They do not go away when the victim leaves. A statistic also showed that a woman leaves an abusive relationship approximately 7 times before she leaves for good.

It is not as easy as walking out and closing the door.

Female, 23

We were moving against each other in the darkness of his room when a sudden bright light exposed us. I was a little tipsy, and I felt myself turn towards the light, laughing and confused. My body tensed up when I realised that it was the flash of his camera as he recorded himself thrusting into me.

There is something very vulnerable about opening yourself up to someone in such an intimate way, and I immediately felt betrayed. It was as if I was naked to the whole world. My body pulled away from him out of instinct.

"It's just for me," he explained, his soft brown eyes creasing at the corners. "For the memories."

Fuelled only by Jameson and diet coke, I felt my muscles loosen up, and I relaxed into him as he continued to record our private moment.

I had nearly forgotten about the whole encounter a few days later when I was in work, however it was soon clear to me that everyone else was aware of it. He worked as a bartender in the restaurant where I waitressed. I leaned over to wipe the tables, and I could feel the eyes of the barmen searing through me, smirking and conspiring together. They made snide comments as they passed me by, their roaming hands grazing the small of my back. I felt myself burn up in their gaze, and in the knowledge that I had been seen in such an intensely private way.

Behind the bathroom door, I let a cry out. I stared into my reflection and felt nothing but disgust at myself for letting someone use me like that. For making me feel that I was simply an object for sexual gratification. And why, deep at my core, did I feel like it was my fault for letting him take the video, not his fault for passing it around like a joint?

> Last year a campaign took off around the country to stop image based sexual abuse. A Change.org petition created by Megan Sims gathered over 84'000 signatures to make image based a criminal offense in Ireland.
>
> Image based sexual abuse is a form of abuse that includes the online posting of sexually explicit visual material without the consent of the person or persons in the material.
>
> This can mean photos or videos that were taken consensually but we're shared with others without all of the parties consent.
>
> In 2018, 561 disclosures of digital abuse and stalking were made to Women's Aid.
>
> In November 2020 tens of thousands of personally explicit images and videos were shared online without consent.
>
> Legislation has been approved that is aimed at tackling the consensual distribution of intimate images with a proposal for a maximum prison sentence of seven to ten sentences. The new legislation will give the guards the tools necessary to ensure those who commit the crimes can be prosecuted.
>
> At the time I am writing this it has just in the last month become a criminal offense.

Male, 24

"I was shocked. I wasn't sure how to react to 'it'. I was angry at the guy, at the guys…. I kind of just wanted to kill someone. She told me every detail. Your kind of left wondering…and you don't want to question it because that's their experience"

When you hear about sexual assault happening to someone you love it's completely different. I was only reading today about a court case; it was about a girl I had worked with and her case got thrown out today because there wasn't enough evidence. But hearing that just didn't feel the same as someone walking you through every step…even though I knew that girl too"

I was 22 and I had a partner who was sexually assaulted just before our relationship began. I don't want to go into too many details because that's her story to tell and not mine. This is just the way it affected me.

We had slept together a few times, we were only starting to see each other but I noticed that she got more distant at times….that I couldn't really touch off her sometimes. It was a couple of months in, I knew about the assault at this stage, and we were having sex and mid sex she jumped up and started crying. I thought I did something wrong.

'It's all going through my head I can feel him on top of me' she said…she cried. That thought drew me in… of being a comparison. Of me being compared to him. In that moment I was that person and usually I was the support. I felt awful, yet the only way I could help her was by staying away from her and then checking in on her the next day. This quickly became a normal routine for us.

. . .

She had no history of seizures before the assault. But then she had these seizures, they were trauma induced seizures. They had calmed down a lot by the time I was dating her though, I'd see her have about four a week I guess...and I would have been seeing her a lot so there wasn't too many I didn't see. This was good for her, after the assault originally, she was having multiple a day.

That's a side to sexual assault that we just don't see. The ongoing affect. The fact that I was watching her live like this daily. Even though I saw her get supports, I never actually saw her get any better. Not just the seizures, I would still see the fear in her eyes in crowds. I had become overly conscious of her mental health, but she was also so conscious of the affect it would have on me. If we were around other male's I noticed myself getting more protective. Going out, being touched by others. I knew all her patterns and routines, what affected her and how she would act around certain people. It definitely did have a toll on me daily, every day I would think 'am I going to be able to be close to her today'. Sometimes something as simple as a hug from her father would trigger a seizure and then that started to happen with me too. Then the time of the year that it had happened, she became distant, I couldn't go near her, couldn't touch her, couldn't have sex, she would get uncomfortable if I was close to her at all.

Throughout the relationship my opinion of her never changed, from before knowing about the assault to after. It definitely made me more protective of her when we were around other men; but I didn't see her differently. There was no hindrance or fault to her. It's not like it was exactly taking a toll on the relationship, it's a part of it but it's not the whole relationships. It's an experience that affects her life that happened before me, I'd have had no reason to not want to go ahead with the relationship. But in the end, it was her who broke it off, it was around the same time as the assault. She said it wasn't fair on me, 'I can't be close to you and I'm pushing you away' she said she needed to be able to sort herself out first. We had been dating for two years.

With my job I'm often in court and see men walk away from cases like this every day. In her case the police knew who it was, but her mental health wasn't good enough. She couldn't go and look at them...a part of me was screaming for her to do something...we can go together I wanted to say...but again, it wasn't my experience, so I never spoke. I felt absolutely infuriated though, not by her but by them. From my own opinion I would have liked to see something happen for her rather than just see her every day and see the effect. I felt that it could be beneficial for her, I hate seeing people get away with this, but I also know that's what normally happens, and I know that seeing that would have torn both her and me to pieces.

Before I experienced this, I would say my experience with rape culture was very black and white...and victimized and brutal. I would never have thought about the aftermaths or the long-lasting affects. I think that the perspective you get when it happens to someone you love is so different, seeing that day in day out...it's not black and white. But we also need to show people that support is there if someone does open up, the numbers aren't there to back up that a person will get help and support if they do speak out. There's no reassurance.

There just isn't enough. What we're doing now to help people, it isn't enough.

Pseudo-seizures are seizures that occur as a response to psychological causes such as mental illness, trauma, abuse. They are also now called psychogenic nonepileptic seizures (PNES)

Pseudo-seizures are not uncommon, according to the Epilepsy Ireland 25% of people who go to hospital to have an EEG (a test that detects electrical activity in your brain, this being an indicator of epilepsy) were having pseudo-seizures rather than epileptic seizures

That means 1 in every 4 people's seizures are due to psychological causes.

70% of people who have pseudo-seizures have experienced physical abuse.

For sexual abuse we only have estimates, the data for sexual abuse has more than likely been hampered by the absence of a clear definition. Or the fact that abuse may have happened young and what happened is unclear. Therefore, it is estimated that between 10% to 77% of people with pseudo-seizures have experiences sexual abuse.

Because the word Pseudo comes from the Latin word meaning false, pseudo-seizures are sometimes mistakenly thought to be fake seizures. Not unlike a lot of mental health issues there was and still is a stigma surrounding pseudo-seizures and their "realness"

Pseudo-seizures are as real as epileptic seizures, they have very similar symptoms – convulsing, jerking, falling down, loss of attention and loss of consciousness.

Unfortunately, a significant difference is that anti-epileptic medication will not help. You just have to wait for the seizure to end. This can last for hours.

Treatment for pseudo-seizures varies from person to person, CBT, counselling, relaxation techniques, eye movement desensitization and reprocessing (EMDR) are a few of the main treatment options.

It's hard to not acknowledge the fact that if people didn't abuse or assault others, then we would have a decrease in disorders like PNES. It's interesting because although many reviews exist about epileptic seizures, there is very little known about the impact of PNES. It's also interesting that it used to be believed that only women were affected by pseudo-seizures. We know now that that's not true, however women are three times more likely to have pseudo-seizures.

We need to know more, we need to stop stigmatizing and as it was so correctly said above, 'what we're doing now to help people, it isn't enough'

Male, 24

I met him on a night out. His friend had tried to wingman for him. Unfortunately, I couldn't follow any of her jokes or even what she was trying to say. She'd had a few too many. He apologised for her, laughing, and bought me a drink. He didn't even mock my fruity cocktail order.

We spent a few nights together, scattered through my second year of college. We had a casual fuck-buddy dynamic. I was nineteen, he was in his early thirties. I always bottomed, and he always topped, which was great. Topping is boring.

One night I went over to his flat.

There was nothing different about him that night. We drank a bit, chatted a little, did some snogging on his balcony. He didn't drink that much, nor did I. Then we went to his bedroom.

I tried to slow things down and he called me stupid. I was pissed. That was mean. Unlike him.

I told him to get off me and he hit me. I was shocked.

I told him I wasn't into kinky stuff. Which was a lie, but how would he know? Our previous encounters had been resoundingly vanilla.

I told him to stop, tried to get up off the bed. He hit me again, harder, and pushed me down.

I tried to push him away, but he was bigger, taller and stronger. Traits I'd previously loved.

He choked me. With the incorrect technique I might add.

I blacked out for a few seconds.

I wouldn't take my underwear off so he tore it open, which in another context might actually have been rather sexy.

I yelled at him and he hit me again. This time a hard blow to the back of the head.

He held me down. Hit me again whenever I tried to get free or moved at all. He told me to "behave".

He called me a pussy when I asked for more lube. I felt very small.

At least he wore a condom. How responsible.

He came on my back. A much bigger load than usual. He had lasted longer too. Been more energetic. For him this was the best sex we'd ever had. He was so turned on.

I remember that. How much he loved it.

He basked in the afterglow.

I got dressed too quickly. I pocketed my socks. I was still wearing the newly assless underwear. My back was still sticky.

My hands were shaking as I put on my shoes.

He noticed. "Why the fuck are your hands shaking?" Why was he so surprised?

I went into the living room. I'd brought a backpack for the beers, I slipped it on.

I headed for the door.

He either grabbed the hood of my hoodie or the handle on top of my backpack. There was a violent jerk, and I feel backwards.

I was sitting on the floor.

He was leaning on the door.

Still naked. Still turned on. Erect again.

He'd never shown this level of stamina, or impressive recovery time, during our normal nights together. In hindsight it's scary that he found this situation so sexy, but at the time it was just confusing.

He came towards me. He wanted a blowjob. He started playing with my hair. I didn't want to make a fuss. I was scared he would start hitting me again, or worse that he would choke me again. Blacking out had been terrifying. What if he accidentally killed me? So, I did what he wanted. He kept telling me to look up at him, but I couldn't. He wasn't gentle. By the end my throat was sore. I swallowed.

He told me to come back to the bedroom. He was holding my face in his hand as he said this, his thumb and forefinger on either cheek, and he was squeezing so hard that the pain was spreading up my teeth and towards my eyes. I didn't say anything, I just nodded and shrugged off my backpack. The fact that I had just given a blowjob while wearing a backpack is such a ridiculous image. It's a nice island of comedy in the middle of this memory.

He headed back towards the bedroom stopping on the way to get something from the fridge. I think it was a bottle of water. Very sensible of him, it's important to stay hydrated. I picked up my backpack, went out the door and softly closed it behind me.

At this point I was quite calm, practical. We were on the sixth floor, I had come up via the lift. I could take the stairs down, but I wasn't sure where the stairwell was. If he followed after me, a stairwell seemed a very secluded spot. I remembered a scene from The Sopranos where a woman was raped at the base of a stairwell and thus, in my infinite wisdom, I concluded that rapists loved stairwells and I should therefore take the lift.

I pressed the button and waited. I could feel his cum on my back and taste it in my mouth. I realised I had some on my face and wiped it away. The lift was clearly visible form his front door. I remember planning possible strategies. I was a little cum-covered Sun Tzu. I was sure he was going to come out after me, but this landing was a public spot, he could hardly drag me back into his flat for fear of me screaming and alerting neighbours. I accepted the possibility that he might follow me into the lift, but how much damage could he do in the thirty or forty seconds in there? Well, I guess he could stab me to death. Dammit, should've hidden his knives. Once I was down in the lobby, I would be safe.

. . .

The lift took too long to arrive. He opened his door. He'd put on some underwear. Fresh underwear I noticed. He was furious. Where was I going? Get back in the flat! Why had I lied to him? I was being a bitch!

The lift came. I tried to step into it. He pulled me back and tried to grab my neck. I pushed him back and turned, my back now facing into the lift. He tried to pull my hair. I slapped his arm away before he could get a proper grip. I started to step backwards into the lift. Then he slapped me. It felt more like a punch. He'd slapped me across the face as hard as he could, much harder than before. My eyes were blurry. I pressed the button. He shouted at me. "Never contact me again, fuck you!". Why was *he* so angry? The lift doors closed.

I was stunned. Annoyed. Mainly embarrassed. In the following days I decided this hadn't happened. My dick had been hard during some of it after all. A misunderstanding. He messaged me a few days later, something silly and friendly. I'd quickly responded. Flirted. I told him I'd had fun the other night. I apologised. We met up again a week later, at his apartment. He locked the door and pocketed the key this time, in fact I think he hid it. I was submissive, obedient. I left in the morning after making him breakfast. It hurt to walk. We met up twice more after that night. When I got home, I would cry and stare into the mirror and scream at myself.

When I finally blocked him on all platforms it wasn't because I had found some inner strength, I was just embarrassed that someone might find out how pathetic I had been.

In 2016, Cliona Saidlear, the head of RCNI said 'worryingly, LGBT survivors can take up to twice as long to report the crime compared with their straight counterparts. They also rely much more on friends and partners and less on parents and family than straight people do. These two findings suggest the potential isolation and added difficulties faced'

In 2013, 4% of survivors attending Rape Crisis Centres for counselling identified as lesbian, gay or bisexual.

Gay males disclosed almost twice the levels of rape of heterosexual males (63% to 34%)

Lesbian, gay and bisexual survivors also disclosed higher levels of multiple incidents of sexual violence than heterosexual survivors.

Although rape does occur much less frequently to men than to women, the incident of male rape is thought to be underreported.

Men who have been raped experience the same similar emotions of anger, denial, shame however most men are taught that they cannot be victims which causes them to have a deeper reluctance to deal with it.

Female, 24

The following is the statement of a female staff member (ND) in relation to an incident of sexual harassment that arose while she was at work. The names, dates, locations and any other identifying information have all been changed to protect the identity of those involved. ND is a 24-year-old female.

Formal Statement from ND
46 Temple Road
12th September 2018

In attendance:

LK – Manager (male)

SM – HR Manager (female)

ND – Staff (female)

SM covered the following introductory points:

- Thanked ND for coming in today
- That we are currently investigating an issue that has come to light in relation to her colleague HP
- This was on foot of a complaint of alleged sexual harassment by HP towards ND, which is alleged to have taken place on the evening of 26th August and into the morning of 27th August 2018
- That if proven HP's actions could potentially be found to be a breach of the code of Conduct and the Dignity at Work Policy.
- SM mentioned that, at this stage, it is important to stress that all matters raised which could potentially be viewed as a breach of the code of conduct are investigated. This does not indicate that the staff member has done anything wrong and no judgement has been passed. Everyone has the right to their good name and due process.
- SM explained that there are a number of people we wish to speak to, to provide further context and background. That is why we have asked to speak with her today.
- SM explained that the investigator's panel's role is to establish the facts.
- SM explained that LK would ask most of the questions and that she (SM) would take notes but may also ask some questions.

- SM said that we will provide ND with a copy of the notes to sign off on.
- SM explained that her statement would be part of the investigation report, which would be sent to HP
- SM explained that to protect all parties involved; it is vital that ND does not discuss outside of this room anything that is covered during this meeting.
- SM said that we recognize that this is a difficult time for ND and reiterated that the counselling services for our employees are available to her.

Questions

LK: We do have a copy of the written complaint that you had made against HP, as well as copies of the texts you had forwarded to your manager. We are going to ask you some questions about the statement and the copies of the text messages.

LK: Could you start by walking us through the events of the evening of 26th August 2018, as you remember them?

ND: HP was the only regular staff on duty that night. Normally the regular staff would remain downstairs as this is the busier floor, but HP actually came upstairs. He kept waiting around. We were seated next to each other in the office at one point and he got really, really close to me. I could feel his leg against mine. He told me that he had feelings for me.

He went downstairs and then came up again for no reason.

. . .

LK: No reason?

ND: Normally he would be on the downstairs floor.

LK: You stated in your complaint that HP has made you feel uncomfortable.

ND: Yes, I actually ended up going for a shower early, because I felt so uncomfortable. When I came out of the shower, he paid me a lot of compliments and asked if my bed was comfortable. He tried to kiss me and grabbed me and then grabbed my bum.

I shouted at him and asked him to get off me. he left. He sent the other staff up to do a job. During the night he tried to call me, but I did not answer.

The next morning, he came up to the office, which would not have been the norm. I had to ask him to leave several times before he did. He was standing in the office rubbing my arm and back. 'Kevin' (another staff member) rang up asking where he was. HP then went downstairs.

LK: Can you describe the set-up of the office. Is it a staff office that converts into a bedroom?

ND: Both the bedroom and bathroom are off of the office.

. . .

LK: So, in order to go from the bathroom and the bedroom one has to enter the office.

ND: Yes.

LK: So, when he kissed you, where was he?

ND: He was in the doorway between the office and the bedroom.

LK: In the thresh hold?

ND: Yes.

LK: I'd like to discuss the texts. We can see that there are three missing from 12:36am, 12:38am and 12:39am on August 27th, 2018. Do you recall what they said?

ND: I never saw them, as I didn't check my phone until the morning and by that time they had been deleted on his end, so I don't know what they said.

LK: We can see from the printout, that there was a video? What was it of?

ND: A song about friends. I don't remember the singer.

. . .

LK: In your complaint you stated that HP had come up the next morning to print out some paperwork?

ND: Yes, that would not have been normal, and I asked him several times to leave. 'Kevin' eventually rang up looking for him.

LK: What happened next?

ND: He did try and contact me by text, but I did not reply.

LK: How did you come to share what happened with AN (another staff member)

ND: I was on shift with her and I eventually broke down and told her what had happened. She told me that she would have to tell the manager as this was very serious. I did not want her to use my name and didn't want to get HP in trouble. I just didn't want to work on the same floor as him again.

LK: What happened then?

ND: AN range me to say that she had told our Leader DG. AN explained that she had not told her it was me, but that DG would be able to look up who was on shift. She said that DG said that this was very serious and would have to be investigated.

. . .

LK: What happened when you met with DG.

ND: I met with both DG and another manager WH. They asked me to write down my account of events, which I did. They offered me counselling, they asked if I was ok to come to work. I said I would be fine as long as I was not in the same place as LK.

He was subsequently moved to another location that night.

Later I was asked to sign the statement and my managers said that it would have to be investigated as it was a serious allegation. So, I decided to make a formal complaint.

LK: Do you have any question for us before we conclude?

ND: Will I know the outcome of the investigation?

SM explained that we would not be sharing the report with her.

ND: Will I have to work with him again?

SM explained that while we would do our best for that not to be the case, we could not guarantee that they would never be rostered on shift together in the future given the fluid nature of shift allocation.

SM thanked ND for coming in today and for providing us with a formal statement. SM reiterated the benefits of our counselling service.

According to the Irish Congress of Trade Unions, four out of five people who experience sexual harassment at work do not report the incident(s).

Out of those who did report, only one in four thought that their report was taken seriously and that it was dealt with to their satisfaction.

But just because workers don't report, it doesn't mean that these incidents don't have a lasting impact. People who have experienced sexual harassment have also reported avoiding certain work situations as a result, that they feel less confident, and a quarter of people reported that it had a negative impact on their mental health.

This is not just a case of "get over it' or "it was only once it won't happen again". These are people's lives', this is how people make a living, these are people who have worked so hard to be working somewhere they love and then to feel unsafe?

What's even more alarming is the abuse of power, one in three workers reported that their own manager or another manager was actually the perpetrator.

And although this is a worldwide problem, Ireland has the highest level of sexual harassment in the workplace in all of Europe.

Sexual harassment can happen to both men and women in the workplace; however, women are more likely to be sexually harassed and to experience higher levels of sexual harassment. Within that, women who are lesbian or bi-sexual and women who are more masculine in behavior, appearance or personality experience sexual harassment at higher rates than other women.

Men who are gay, transgender, petite or just not "man enough" encounter more harassment than other men.

Another strong factor for the lack of reporting in relation to this, and which was shown well in ND's case is the fact that reporting can be stigmatized, humiliating when not taken seriously and in ND's case, although it was her case, she would not even find out the outcome of the investigation. Which offers no reassurance or solution and would make a person think, why? Why did I go through this interview and tell management and other staff only for it to all be for nothing?

Another factor that contributes to sexual harassment in work is the work environment, women who work in environments in which men outnumber women, if management is male-led, women experience more frequent incidents of sexual harassment.

Every workplace is different but that shouldn't make a difference to an individual's right to feel safe and secure in their place of work.

Female, 27

When I was 9/10 years old, I lived with my mum and my mum's boyfriend. From what I remember, everything was fine at first. It felt like a normal childhood but they used to fight a lot so mum and I would have to find other places to stay. As a kid, you have many questions about how the world works and some of those questions involve things about the birds and the bee's, how babies are made and just how the world works around the sexual nature. As my mum worked a lot, the only person I could ask these questions to as a curious child was him. My mum's boyfriend. I heard my friends talking about sex in primary school and I didn't understand a lot of what they were saying. Since I was an only child I had never heard of these things before. So, when I got home from school one day I asked him what sex was and why people do it. He said to me that it would make more sense if he showed me. He took me to my bedroom. I still remember my quilt, the colours of my curtains, the way the house was set up. He laid me on my bed and said to me this is the part where women have sex, then he pulled my pants down and he grabbed my hand and made me touch myself 'where women have sex'. He then stood up, took off his pants, lied down on the bed, pointed to his penis and said that this is what men use to have sex. When I said that I was confused, he said he would show me how good sex feels and that's why people have sex because of how good it feels. He then grabbed my hand, put it on himself and told me to go up and down in a slow motion. When I said I didn't like it, he put his hand around my hand and didn't let me let go. He then kept going, in that up and down motion until he showed me what happens when men have sex. I said I didn't like it and I wanted it to stop, but he then said well it feels good for women too and I shall show you why. When I asked if this was all okay, and if mum would be mad, he said it was okay because this is how children learn about the birds and the bees. When I'm thinking about it now, I was an idiot to believe him, but I was too young to sense that anything was wrong. He then went on to show me why women have sex, he laid me down on my pink bed, he made me open my legs, holding each one open, and he touched me to show me where women have sex. He then went to explain that women can make themselves feel good as well on their own, and forcefully used my hand, more accurately my finger, to touch myself, to show me how that is. I don't remember anything else after that, I remember him telling me not to tell my mum, but to this day I don't know why I didn't think that something might be wrong.

A couple of years went by, and I'd forgotten all about it, we moved to a different city, to a different part of the country, to a different school with new friends and I went about life just being a child. Mum and he continued to have fights regularly until one day she said enough was enough and she left him. We found our own home, and we just moved on. Sometime later, I'm not sure how long, I think I was 14/15, I was in class at school and an announcement came through to tell me that she was here to pick me up, which was completely out of the blue. When I walked to reception, he was there with my mum waiting for me. I don't remember asking why he was there. I guess I just thought he was there for a visit or just to say hello, as he was the closest thing to a father figure that I had. He stayed with us at our house for I don't know how long, but I went about my childhood. I had friends over, I still went to school just like a normal child, and then out of the blue one day he left, and I never saw him again.

Again, a couple of year later, when I was around 16, I got home from school and mum told me that there were two female police officers that were going to come and talk to me. I didn't know what this was about, but they came in and sat me down at the dinner table and began to ask me questions about him. If I'm honest I thought they came to get at me because I hadn't done my homework or something silly, but when they started asking me about him, I don't know why, but I said that he was fine. That he was a good stepdad, that we had heaps of fun when I was growing up. When the female officers left, I asked my mum why they were asking questions about him. At first she refused to tell me, but I broke her down and she eventually told me that he was being investigated for some things that he had done to children. The second my mum told me that, it was almost like the big bang had happened in my head. Everything suddenly clicked and I started to remember things that I hadn't thought about in years. I felt awful for not telling the female officers what I remembered because I was fighting with myself wondering if it was something I had made up as a kid or if it was something so awful that I had suppressed all this time until someone made me remember. I didn't tell my mum, because I didn't know how to have that conversation with her, I had just told all these police officers that it was just fine, and I would have looked like an idiot going back on what I had just said, even though I had only just remembered what had happened all those years ago.

A couple of days later, when I realised that's what had happened to me and I wasn't just a child mistaking thing, I spoke to my best friend Noah about it. We laid on the trampoline in my back yard like we used to as kids and I completely opened up to him and asked him what I should do. He told me that what happened isn't right and that I needed to come forward with what really happened. I didn't speak to anyone else about this until a couple of years later. I guess I never had the courage to open up about what happened to me, I was scared someone would judge me and I was scared that my mum would find out as I didn't want to get into trouble. But as a young teenager, starting relationships and having boyfriends and doing what teenagers do, I realised I couldn't trust anyone and I was scared to be physical with anyone. I realised that I was actually a lot more scared by what had happened to me than I thought. That's when I decided I needed to tell the truth about what had happened. I remember going to the dentist one day. I don't know why but that was the day I got the courage to tell my mum. I told her in the car on the way back home and I will never forget the look on her face that she had that day. She didn't say anything to me apart from that she was very sorry and that we needed to have a bigger talk about this when we got home When we got home, mum sat me down at the table and in depth told me the reasons why he was being investigated. I found out that he was being charged all over the country for multiple cases of child pornography and that multiple videos found were videos of myself and my friends just having a shower at sleepovers, or just us sleeping, or going to the toilet. They were all filmed that time he surprised me after school before he took off for the last time. Mum told me that my friends then had to go to the police station and prove it was them in the videos by taking in the pyjamas in the videos, and they are now friends that no longer speak to me or want anything to do with me because of the man my mum let into our house. Mum told me that whenever I am ready, I needed to go and tell the truth to the investigation team about what happened to me and she got me in contact with the lead investigator who was dealing with the cases. Myself, my mum and my friend Noah all went to the police station a couple of weeks later to provide statements of what happened and when I started remembering things. I gave exact details on the floor plan of the house we lived in at the time, the clothing he was wearing, and I was wearing because all of a sudden, I could remember every little detail and it's something that never ever leaves my thoughts. And it took me a long time to not be angry at myself for suppressing what happened to me. After the investigation was carried out, I was told that there was nothing they could do. He couldn't be charged for what he did to me because I couldn't provide any evidence and he had already served jail time for such cases like mine. I was so angry that I couldn't get the justice I deserved. I was angry about the constant flashbacks and effects it had on my relationships. I was angry that the trauma it caused me is something I have to bear on my own. It took me a very long time to find the strength in myself to accept the fact that I wasn't going to get justice. But I figured out that what I can get, that is 100x better, is self-worth that no one including him could break. Even though I didn't get revenge because I told the truth too late, it doesn't mean that my life is over. It doesn't mean that the investigation system has done me wrong, but what it does mean is that I can now be a stronger, more empowered woman that I have ever been. And I feel free now I no longer have to keep that burden on my chest. The reason I feel like it's so important to share my story is because I want anyone who has been through anything like this to believe in themselves to know if something is wrong and to speak up even if you have doubts that what happened to you wasn't right. If you ever have a bad feeling about someone, if you ever don't feel comfortable, it is okay to speak up. Someone will listen, and there is going to be a million people to hold your hand and help you. And just because there might not always be punishment for those that deserve it, doesn't mean you can't find justice in yourself to be a more complete you and live a happier life away from what hurt you in the first place.

Female, 23

It took a long time for me to understand what had happened. That my dad sexually abused me when I was a little girl. I buried all my memories and feelings.

I was just a little girl and something so painful...it became so disorganized and hidden. But the effect of that only grows as you get older, or at least that's what happened for me.

The self-doubt and the lack of self-esteem which led to anxiety and terrible depression all stemmed from these instances of his misuse of power and the breaking of trust.

This disgusting behavior is so hard to associate with the man who also helped me learn to ride a bike.

I think there's a lot of loneliness in holding the knowledge of sexual abuse.

This person is in the community, and he is popular and kind and an intelligent person. Yet he also has a lot of other behaviors that are almost unforgivable?

Trying to make sense of how a predator and a Dad can be the same person?

And then of course, the doubt of others believing me.

Just that abuse of power...it really messes with your mind.

Thankfully I could get the help I needed, and with good friends I could learn to nurture a better sense of trust.

But the impact of a man being manipulative and committing sexual abuse is just so horrible and can so easily goes unnoticed. You face so much doubt, not only from your community but even within yourself....because...how could someone do something like that?

Tusla is a statutory organisation developed to support and promote the development, welfare and protection of children.

In 2018, Tusla received 67 child protection referrals every day.

3'548 referrals were made concerning children suffering sexual abuse. That's three and a half thousand people (give or take for someone who abuses multiple children) who are sexually abusing a child. That's also only the ones we are aware of.

According to an INMO article, the most common form of sexual abuse is incest, most frequently being father-daughter relationships. This results in a child to feel confusion about their self- worth and it will also have a knock on affect in their relationships with other people.

Almost 80% of children who have suffered sexual abuse were abused by someone they knew. The other percentage is made up of those in authority such as a teacher or coach (12%), other (5%) and strangers being the lowest of all at 3%.

A SAVI report found that most abuse occurred before the age of 12. That being 67% of females and 62% of males abused before the age of 12. This SAVI report also indicated that people who were sexually abused as a child were 8 times more likely to have an inpatient stay in a psychiatric hospital.

Around one third of sex offenses against children are committed by minors – 93% are brothers abusing younger sisters. Behaviours include fondling, unwanted sexual advances or forcing siblings to view porn.

The effects of sibling abuse are alike to parent-child abuse and have a long term negative impact. Victims of all ages can experience shame, guilt and anxiety.

It confuses boundaries and what equals a healthy relationship. So much of our adult behaviour is shaped when we are a child and therefore pleasing behaviours to avoid conflict may become an adults normal.

Childhood sexual abuse is a huge underbelly in our world and like many survivors say 'it can so easily go un-noticed'

Female, 22

People usually think that when a boy pays attention to them, it means that you're "pretty" or people find you attractive. Girls are taught that the piercing male gaze and the wolf whistles are good things and to be proud of your beauty. As I've grown up in a male dominated world, I've realised this is so wrong. I'm sure every girl at some point has had the experience of a man making sexual comments or touching them inappropriately in a club or at a party and felt shame and disgust, yet no one bats an eyelid at this. I was walking home from the train station only last week, when a car full of men stopped beside me and were shouting and cat-calling me and yet I was the one to feel embarrassed? I cried the rest of the way home as I realised that this harmful "boys will be boys" narrative is fuelling the hate and misogyny towards women. No one would take me seriously if I told them the reason I was upset was because a car full of teenagers shouted at me. They would think I was a "snowflake" or that I should have taken it as a compliment. This is what's wrong with our society today and how women are viewed, doing something as mundane walking home from the train station.

Female, 22

I was very lucky. I was 16 years old, walking back to school from the dentist when it started raining. I was just in my uniform. This man pulled up beside me, late 50s early 60s, driving some fancy BMW. He was wearing a beige suede coat with a thick wool lining. Walking alone I was pretty scared of people but always worried I was being rude. He pulled up right beside me, smiled brightly and said I looked like I was getting soaked, asked if I wanted a lift. I said I was fine and thanked him, the school was 2 minutes away. He kept insisting and I kept saying I was fine. After a bit of back and forth I just remember his face twist a bit and he got out of the car. He came around and opened the passenger door, smiling again and said something like "ah come on you're already soaked". All I remember thinking is 'don't be rude'. How bad will this man feel if I tell him I'm scared? I started panicking inside and next thing I remember I'm in the car. I didn't know why I got in. I was 16. I just knew I didn't want to be rude.

He locked the doors as soon as I got in, then straight away asked me my age. He kept touching a bruise on my leg asking if I was okay, telling me I was beautiful. I was very aware of my skirt. He drove so slowly. I kind of flipped into robot survival mode – playing innocent while scouting for a way out. I was 100% certain I was getting kidnapped, there was no way for me to unlock the door and he was definitely stronger than me. I was very aware of what he could potentially do and I did not want to set him off. He told me I was beautiful again. I thanked him. He was talking to me as if we were old friends, he kept saying my name.

We very slowly came to the school. I was convinced he was just going to drive by but by the grace of whatever was looking out for me that day he pulled in. He still wasn't letting me out though. He didn't unlock the car until I said we could see each other again then he relaxed, unlocked the doors and as he reached for his phone I just leapt out of the car.

My school was very particular about their one way parking system. He had driven in the wrong way so I knew my principal would be straight out to say it to me. I didn't want to tell him, it wasn't any of his business and I didn't think it was a huge deal. He let me out of the car, didn't he?

I must have been in shock because just as he drove away I remember saying to my principal "I don't know that man" and laughing hysterically. He told me he had to call the police, then I started to cry. I didn't want to talk to them. Nothing had happened, I got in the car I got out of the car and then I was at school. It felt like my fault. My principal kept pointing out to the guards and my parents (who I also begged him not to call) that I only started crying when he said he was calling the guards. Everyone wanted to know why I was so silly to get into the car, nobody told me he was wrong to pressure me to. They just kept asking why I got in the car. My principal sent the vice principal in to ask if the man had touched me – she said he was too embarrassed to ask. I immediately said no and she told me to have a more respectful tone. I don't remember a lot after that I just shut down. I just remember sitting in the principal's office with all of these men standing over me, I couldn't understand why that upset me.

Women are raised to be frightened of men but also that they are our protectors. Every girl is told stories about scary men, never talk to strange men, don't trust men you don't know and if you feel threatened by a man you should find a different better man to protect you. I was never taught how to say I was uncomfortable. I didn't think I was entitled to boundaries because I was never given them.

I know now why I got in the car – because if I didn't he would have made me. I knew the moment I saw his face turn that this man could very easily get me in that car. I was actually grateful to him for not raping me. For a long time I was thankful that it was him and not someone angrier. The guards said he drove by the school twice that day and once the day after. I never got upset about it after that. I laughed when I said it to my friends. I was very grateful after that to be in an all-girls school, girls understood that it was scary, but that it could have been so much worse. Nothing bonds teenage girls like creepy men. They knew what I knew – that I was very lucky.

Female, 23

I was only 17 when you decided that it was ok for you to try and touch me. Without my permission. You decided that my voice didn't matter. Without acknowledging my constant no's and without acknowledging my hands telling you where to keep your own. This game we have to play as women, purely for their sexual gratification. That if we say yes we are easy sluts and if we say no we are frigid and boring. We need to stop teaching our girls to lie and say 'I have a boyfriend' and stop telling them to change how they dress - this alone implying it's our fault, and we must have put ourselves in this position, because how dare we think men could have any self-control at the sight of skin? Instead, we need to start teaching our boys what respectful, consensual sex is. We need to educate them that no means no, full stop. We have to stop assuming, blaming and victimising. I was only 17 when I was made to feel like my voice did not matter.

Female, 22

I have found countless reasons to blame myself for what happened that night. I tell myself that I shouldn't have gone out. I shouldn't have drank. I shouldn't have worn that top. I shouldn't have spoken to him.

I should have been more careful.

I don't speak to myself in the same way I would speak to a friend if it happened to her. No matter how hard I try, I still believe it was my fault.

It's been nearly four years since I was sexually assaulted by someone I thought I could trust. Although I don't have much memory of the actual assault, it has affected my life in many ways. It has provoked random spells of anxiety in my everyday life. It has spoiled intimate relationships. It has also made me a very untrusting and cynical person when meeting new people.

I still blame myself for choosing to go out that night, for not sticking with my friends and for letting my guard down. He knew I wasn't interested in him. I had been subject to unwanted attention off him previous to that night. My last memory is seeing him standing at the bar. At some stage, something was put into my drink.

Casual dating and 'one-night stand' culture has made it so difficult for rape victims. It's not possible to give consent when you are under the influence of alcohol. People make you believe that if you chose to drink, you were asking for something to happen and you were not being careful enough. This is victim blaming and it makes it very difficult for victims to heal. There is only one cause of rape. Rapists.

I have carried the pain of this assault with me since the night it happened. I regularly go over what I could have done differently to prevent it from happening. I hope someday I will heal from it and move forward.

> Victim blaming is the attitude which suggest that the victim rather than the perpetrator bears responsibility for the assault. Victim blaming occurs when it is assumed that an individual did something to provoke the actions or words of the perpetrator.
>
> In saying this it seems unreasonable and unrealistic as to why anyone could or would ever blame the victim of a sexual assault but if we think about it a bit more we might realize that victim blaming in cases of sexual assault has become so engrained that we may not even realize it is happening.
>
> Examples of victim blaming can include
>
> - You shouldn't have been drinking
> - You must have sent mixed messages
> - What were you wearing?
> - How hard did you try to stop it?
> - Why didn't you come forward sooner?
> - You must have known what was going to happen if you went there with him?
>
> The worst part is that victim blaming is not only used in personal lives, but is widely used as a weapon in courtrooms and more often than not victims are blamed in the media.

It is thought that victim blaming may have come about to make people feel better about themselves. It is much safer and easier for people to imagine that the victims did something wrong. That they must have done something in order for this to happen to them. This works for some people as it can be very scary to think that this can in fact just happen to anyone. Which is the true case.

But for some people victim blaming means they can convince themselves that they would be able to prevent this or protect themselves or their loved ones from this happening to them.

It helps people to feel like the world is safe but in reality it harms the victim even more.

There is a psychological experiment from 1966 that tries to explain victim blaming. In this study a large group of women were to watch another women as she received painful electric shocks. The woman wasn't actually receiving any shocks and was an actress but the other woman believed she was getting shocked every time she got an answer wrong.

The women were upset as they saw the victim suffer, then some of them were offered to stop the shocks when the victim got the answer wrong but they choose to compensate the victim with money as a reward for when she got answers right.

The other group of women were not able to do anything and they watched the victim continue to get shocked with no way of helping.

The results were incredible, the group of women who gave her money as a reward saw this woman as a good person. While the women who watched the women be shocked continuously were more likely to see her as a bad person who deserved this punishment.

It was concluded that the women who couldn't help the victim felt that they must see her as a bad person in order for them to continue to see the world as just and fair. If they convinced themselves she was a bad person they would not be as affected by her suffering.

Blaming the victim helps to maintain a positive view of the world. But it is a false belief.

Victims blame themselves for similar reasons. They too also want to believe the world is safe and perhaps 'if I dressed more conservatively, this won't happen to me again'

Victim blaming has made it much more difficult for victims to come forward or report.

It also reinforced predator behaviour. It means perpetrators avid accountability and responsibility for their actions.

Sexual assault is never the victims fault. It is always the perpetrators fault and as a society it is our responsibility to start questioning our own automatic thoughts.

Female, 23

From what I can think of off the top of my head

- One time when I was volunteering on this farm in Israel. It was after a big party, one of the other volunteers that I'd never even spoken to before followed me into the girls shared bathroom and tried to grab me and kiss me while I was brushing my teeth. Luckily he didn't follow me when I ran out.
- I was in student accommodation last year and this guy who was flat mates with my friend came to drink with

me and my friends in the communal area. He was giving me drinks and we ended up back in my room. I don't remember what happened. I was the most blackout drunk I've ever been in my life. I don't think there was a condom involved but I didn't even remember enough to be sure. I took the morning after pill the next day anyways. I then heard from my friend that he complained about me being too drunk.
- In Brussels the harassment is really bad, from the age of thirteen on you'll have fifty-year-old men cat calling you on the street and coming up to you trying to stroke your hair. I have never been on one night out there without one creepy incident happening.
- When I was in Paris this guy that was around 10 years older than me bought drinks for me and my friends in a bar. Then when he tried to follow us home and kiss me, my friend told him to fuck off and he said 'but I paid for you'

Female 21

A friend of mine and me were at a party and there were loads of lads and only three of us girls. My friend got really drunk really fast and started vomiting and she passed out in a bed. She woke up and a lad was kissing her and was feeling her up down below. She said that she was so asleep and still so drunk that she thinks she just thought it was normal and went along with it but it was only the next day that she realized how bad it was. There was also vomit in the bed, he knew the state that she was in. When I said it to the boys the next day they all just laughed at it.

. . .

Another time, I brought a boy home. I was very drunk so I got into bed and tried to go to sleep. He kept trying to kiss me for ages so eventually I kissed him back for a second. I then said to him that I was too tired and wanted to go to sleep and he said 'no you can't do that, you've made me hard now you need to help'. I think I looked at him in disgust and told him to get out but it just shows you what some boys/girls will try.

I've had this experience a few times where lads are like 'aw you have to help me out now you've made me horny'

A male friend of mine told me he woke up after a one night stand to the girl giving him head. He said he freaked out and he went along with it but just shows you how it happens to everyone.

Male, 22

This situation happened when I was 18 years old. I was at a Leaving Cert results party and, as young people are prone to do at that age, got quite drunk. Over the night, myself and a girl got particularly close to each other and we started kissing. After a while, we moved upstairs to one of the empty bedrooms in the house. Things were getting more heated and we started messing around a bit. This was a fairly big deal for me at the time because I hadn't done anything sexual with somebody for a while after a nasty breakup.

While hooking up, I started realizing how drunk we both were. This, alongside my relationship history, made me start to feel uncomfortable with where things were heading. We had barely said a word to each other after closing the bedroom door, so I didn't want to ruin the mood by speaking out. I had also seemed very enthused up to this point, so I felt almost as if I couldn't retract myself at this stage. After a few minutes, the girl got on top of me and we started having sex. This was what prompted me to finally speak up, and I told her to stop and that I didn't want to. The girl immediately got off me and apologized profusely. I told her it was ok, and that I had made it confusing for her to read whether I wanted to or not.

I realize my experience is nowhere near as upsetting as what many others have been through, and that being a male immeasurably reduces one's likelihood of being sexually assaulted in our society. However, it has taught me the importance of being clear and verbal when being intimate with others. I have never told anyone this story. It isn't traumatic or embarrassing, but it has stuck with me in a very personal way. In that instance, I had a brief idea of what could have happened if the girl hadn't stopped, or if I had never said anything at all. This made me realize how much more common cases of sexual assault are than I initially thought.

Consent is always required in a situation and should be asked if not made very obvious. If you're comfortable enough to get intimate with someone, you should be able to ask a simple, "Are you ok with this?".

In 2016 a EU wide survey showed that 21% of Irish people believed having sex without consent can be justified in certain situations.

In this survey respondents were asked the following question

"Some people believe that having sexual intercourse without consent may be justified in certain situations. Do you think this applies to the following situations.

I decided to have a read of this full report and to say I was shocked is an understatement.

This poll found that 11% of Irish people believed that being on drugs or drunk could justify sex without consent and a shocking 9% think it's okay if a person voluntarily goes home with someone. 7% of Irish people also believe it is justified if the person is out walking alone at night.

10% of Europeans think a lack of consent is justified if a person doesn't clearly say no or physically fight back and 7% believe it is justified if there was flirting beforehand or if the person has several sexual partners.

It's actually heart-breaking to write those statistics out and realize they came from real humans that are walking around. That they are not just numbers on a page. These are peoples family and friends. To think that 1 in every 10 people believes being drunk justifies sex without consent is absolutely horrible to think about and just shows how far we need to go.

Consent is permission for something to happen or an agreement to do something. One of the most concerning thoughts about our current understanding of consent is that it possible for one person to leave a sexual encounter and to think it was consensual and another will leave it believing they were assaulted. This indicates that our education around consent is lacking and unclear.

In the Republic of Ireland, the legal definition of consent in The Criminal Law (Sexual Offences) Act 2017 states that "a person consents to a sexual act if he or she freely and voluntarily agrees to engage in that act' and it also provides circumstances in which consent cannot be given, one of these is being impaired by alcohol or drugs.

Now when we compare that to the fact that 11% of Irish people believe that being drunk can justify sex without consent we not only see how there is a lack of awareness around consent but the fact is that what they are saying they think is okay is actually illegal.

Female 24

I once remember that I was at a party. There was this really insistent boy that was saying he wanted to make out with me. He kept talking but I ignored him and then he started to touch my ass. He wouldn't stop so I had to ask a friend to pretend to be my boyfriend just so that the boy would stop bothering and touching me.

Female, 24

When I was 18, I moved to Dublin from Toronto to go to medical school. I didn't know anyone at all when I arrived. One night during fresher's week we went out to the clubs. I had drunk too much, and I wasn't allowed into the club. All of the people I had come out with had gotten in and didn't notice that I hadn't. I texted some of the friends I had met that week and waited for them to come and meet me outside the club.

While I was waiting outside; a noticeably older, intoxicated man in his 30's approached me and started talking to me. I tried to ignore him, but he kept talking to me. I was eighteen, in a foreign country and I remember being nervous that he might make a scene if I kept ignoring him, so I thought 'what's the harm in talking to him while I wait a couple of minutes for my friends'

While we were talking, I remember feeling uncomfortable and scanning the door of the club every few seconds to search for my friends.

The man started asking very personal questions about me and at some point, he had inched his way extremely close to me. He then reached out and started touching my breasts.

I pushed his hands away and yelled at him. He continued to try and grab my breast while talking about then in a very dehumanizing way.

He got uncomfortable then when raising my voice started to draw other people's attention towards us and he walked away. He then proceeded to stand across the street and stare at me.

I immediately called my friends crying and thankfully they were outside within seconds.

The Garda happened to be outside the club shortly thereafter and I approached them to tell them what had happened as the man was still sitting across the street staring at me and I was afraid that he would prey on me again or try to do something similar to another girl. Unfortunately, the Garda couldn't do much and just asked him to leave.

Fortunately, nothing worse happened that night, although I recognize that it easily could have. I remember feeling helpless, while simultaneously feeling as if it was my own fault. I felt that if I hadn't drank as much or just kept ignoring him that I could have avoided the entire situation. I know now how far from the truth that feeling was.

I wish I could say this was the last time something like that happened but unfortunately it wasn't.

One day I hope that when asked to share our stories there won't be so many to choose from.

Female, 22

I was about 17 years old and it was in a night club. I was out with my friends but I had lost them so I went to the dance floor looking for them. I wasn't drunk but I had been drinking.

Suddenly this guy came up behind me guy and just started fingering me from behind, he gobbed me and walked away. I didn't know who it was because it was dark and the lights were all flashy and he was wearing a hat so I couldn't see much. I sort of stood there in shock and then I saw my friend at the bar so I ran over to her and they took me away from the dance floor area.

Female, 21

I was on sixth year holiday with a few friends in Greece and were in a club and were all having a great time just dancing away. Then I kind of noticed a group of lads eyeing us up but wasn't interested so did the typical girl thing of not making eye contact and making your friend circle tighter. Show you're not interested but don't offend.

However, the guys were still kind of lingering around us and we continued to pay them no mind until one of them stuck his hand up my dress and tried to grab my vagina.

I don't even remember if he succeeded in getting that far as I spun around and shoved my hand against his chest, gave him a death stare and grabbed the girls to leave.

I don't think I've ever felt so deeply angry in my life.

The girls didn't know anything had happen until we left and I told them.

Female, 33

Two years ago I was in a popular venue enjoying myself on this huge crowded dance floor area with a friend. We had been dancing for hours and enjoying the music. She wanted to go to the bathrooms so I said I would wait on the dance floor because I was loving the song that was on and I was happy bopping around.

A guy came up to me, shouting over the music into my ear trying to ask me something. He asked me why I was on my own. I didn't take too much notice of him and just said that my friend was in the bathroom and I had wanted to stay and dance to the song. He kept asking me why I did that. He said that it was so strange that I stayed on my own because "girls always go to the bathroom together". I kind of continued to say the same answer again, because sometimes when you're on your own you feel you owe these guys something, an answer... I don't know why.

What happened next happened fast. I wasn't sure if it actually happened, but I also knew that it did. He shouted "Why didn't you go with her to the bathrooms- are you a man or something!?" and grabbed my crotch area, pretty hard. I can't remember what I did because I was shocked, but I know I stood back and he just carried on chatting to his friends as if nothing had happened at all. My friend came back and I said "I think something strange just happened, but I don't know if it's a big deal or not". She was concerned and angry and said that she was going to say something to him. I felt really embarrassed, which makes me feel sad now. I almost started to second guess if it was real, because he was just acting completely normal chatting to his friends one second later after the incident. Yet I was just left there standing still trying to make sense of what just happened. But I could feel exactly where he had grabbed me, so I knew it was real. She confronted him, and he came back up to me shouting in my face calling me a liar. I told him that I was fine (I don't think I was) but that he should never do that to another girl in the future. I told him it's not ok to grab someone like that. He continued to shout and become more and more aggressive calling me a liar again. We then proceeded to tell the bouncer, who was so nice and supportive about it. He literally found the guy in the huge crowd, lifted him up, and kicked him out. What baffles me now is the fact that I felt embarrassed for even making "a big deal" out of it at the time. It was a hundred percent a form of sexual assault, and there's no shame in confronting and being upset by a situation like that.

> Perpetrators in nightclubs and outside nightclubs rely on the silence of others. They rely on the likeability that anyone who see's something they do, or see something that doesn't seem quite right, that they won't say anything or do anything because really "it's none of their business"
>
> Dr. Cliona Saidlear, executive director of the Rape Crisis Network Ireland said "If you're in a pub, night-club, street, school corridor, grabbing people (particularly women) by their bum or crotch has become more common"
>
> It is a sad fact that I'm sure many women will agree with that they have not themselves or know someone who has been grabbed on a night out. It is so commonly accepted.
>
> Dr. Saidlear also said "If we don't pay attention to where the bar is, it keeps raising and only gets more and more serious" and "it's more important that we notice it at a lower bar because this is where it's safer to name it and intervene, to say I'm not okay with that I see"
>
> As was said above, without external supports such as friends and bouncers who intervene a situation like this can become intimidating quickly. It can also become even more dangerous quickly.
>
> If you were in your local shops and someone walked past and groped you from behind you would be shocked. And yes, some people are justifiably still shocked when it happens on a night out, but we have an expectation of it. I know myself as females we are sometimes more hesitant to even say anything as I could just make the situation worse

or result in getting kicked out ourselves. Groping and grinding can often be viewed as a "joke" and "a compliment". But these incidents would be unacceptable outside of a nightclub or bar setting. This results in creating an environment that is unequal in how safe a gender feels whilst in it. A female should be able to be on a dance floor alone without being harassed, because we would never even question leaving a male alone on a dance floor. We wouldn't question a male alone outside a nightclub waiting for someone.

A survey done by the Macquarie University Law Society found that 13% of people said they were fearful every time they went out as a result of unwanted sexual harassment, while 50% of people said they felt this fear some of the time. In this same survey most believed that staff and security did not respond adequately to complaints of sexual harassment.

Whilst researching for this piece, I came across an article which I'm not going to name specifically.

It was basically a list of advice and tips for girls to have a good safe night out.

"it included lines like "make sure your friends know where you are at all times" and "instead of shouting and starting a huge scene, using a safe word can come in handy" and "it's not cool to be that sloppy drunk so know your limits" and my ultimate favorite "Wear reasonable clothes" This article was not old. It was written in the last five years and the emphasis was still on the female taking responsibility for what a man could potentially do.

Naturally I decided to see if there was any advice for men on how to have a safe night out. As I'm sure you guessed there was no guideline for a safe night out for men. I googled and googled. However, there was articles and advice that were not directed at a certain gender, general advice of staying in well-lit areas and watching you drink. But no articles aimed specifically at men.

Of course, there is benefits to knowing some tips to stay safe on a night out. Just because we don't want a problem to be there, it doesn't mean we completely ignore the fact that it clearly is. However, suggesting that something like what we wear or that we should not cause a scene if someone does something inappropriate only feeds into the cycle of victim blaming and silencing victims.

Female, 22

I feel that the stereotype that men everywhere are predators has been placed on us and them by society. Being a girl, I am always told don't dress too revealingly, don't get too drunk, don't go on dates without having an escape plan. This can be exhausting. I specifically get told that I am too reckless that I will just jump into anyone's car or go to anyone's house without much precaution. I **enjoy** meeting new people! I **enjoy** dating! These are all things that should be okay for me to enjoy without having a fear of being murdered or raped.

Even though these are risks, and strange men have approached me and said strange things and random guys in bars have felt that they had the need and the right to grab my ass without thought, they don't intimidate me. This is because everyone who has raped me or assaulted me has been somebody I knew, I cared about, and I loved. One of the men that assaulted me was a dear friend of mine. We got lunch every day; we were always in each other's company and really boosted each other up. On a night out, he got too drunk, and revealed that he had feelings for me. I had the audacity to not feel the same way. In response, he grabbed every part of my body and tried to kiss me and feel me up and pushed me into a wall after I said what I said, to which I pushed him away and ran off. Even though that night made me extremely uncomfortable the worst part of that endeavour is that when probed about the night he refused to believe me even though he had no recollection of the night and completely invalidated the trauma that had so clearly distressed me.

When I found out my ex-boyfriend was going to be at the same party I was going to that evening, I was nervous (to say the least). I did what anyone in their early twenties would do in this situation - I drank a **lot**. This resulted in me approaching him and starting a conversation, an example of my inner genius. I don't remember much else. I recall him being way more sober than me at the time. I'm not going to try and argue that he was fully to blame, as I don't remember enough of the party to know. It's pretty likely that I made a move on him because he was comfortable, and familiar but when I woke up, it was a different story entirely. I woke up in his bed, naked. Not knowing how or why I was there, I asked. He responded that we had "obviously" had sex. He then proceeded to ask me to leave. Unlike the first occurrence, this one has developed in my head as time has progressed. I left his house hungover and ill, and just tried to accept that what had happened was in the past. When I gave it more thought (when I was in a clearer state of mind), I considered the fact that I must have been unconscious if I can't remember any of the events and wasn't able to make decisions about my consent. When asking my friends for their opinions about what had happened, they disregarded it by saying he was my boyfriend before, that I'd slept with him in the past, and therefore what he had done was fine. As I got older and wiser, I realised that they were wrong. I did not consent. If I can't remember the events, how could I have possibly agreed to partake in them? All I knew was that I felt disgusting, that no one would ever believe me, and I would just have to deal with the trauma that these people, that I loved, had forced upon me

Female, 22

When I was 16 I went to a close friends party - all people who were invited I knew and I was comfortable with to set the scene. We were all drinking. The boy who I liked at the time (actually one of my closest guy friends) - something had changed between us at school over the last few months we were very close to officially dating. Basically we hooked up at the party away from the rest of the people at the party. I told him in advance that I didn't want to have sex because I was on my period at the time. He proceeded to pressure me trying to unzip my pants while on top of me and convince me otherwise despite me saying no and stop. This would have been my first time and also his and I didn't want it to happen under those circumstances. Anyways I somehow managed to push him off me and said I wanted to return to the party. At this point my friend had come to look for me. I went back to the party with her and to the bathroom. After seeing that he wasn't back at the party I wanted to go check if he was okay as he was pretty drunk and I'd left him alone. Anyways o found him asked him if he was okay and he told me to "fuck off you c*!t".

Female, 22

I was too polite to you in the smoking area. Maybe I liked the attention or maybe I was too scared to explicitly say no.

I don't like attention anymore.

You bought me a drink. I barely remember the actual drinking of it- it's a whisper kind of memory; barely there, the last tangible event before blackout.

It was morning then and I woke up in my bed. There was vomit all over me, thick chunks clinging to my damp hair. I was shameful. I was always falling asleep when I drank. Something about the cocktail of wine and sertraline was instantly sedative. I could not believe I'd just sent myself home and got sick, what a waste of a night, the girls will probably find it funny though. Imagine not remembering coming home, chronic.

I looked at my phone – I had a text telling me that I needed to buy the morning after pill, that you hadn't used a condom.

More vomit.

The feeling clung to me. The feeling of my own shame, my own stupidity. I was always so stupid with boys. Always too drunk. Always too pliable. Too easy.

You texted again - I'd been really good. I was so sexy - would I want to do that again sometime? I did not reply. You called me a bitch. Said I'd been all talk the night before.

I alternated between jest - ha can't believe I rode him- to fierce denial - no stop that's not funny what are you talking about, do not ask me about that, I won't talk about it shut up shut up shut up.

I have grown to regard the events of that night with detachment. I sometimes find this concerning, but that did not happen to me - it was a different girl.

If it happened to another girl it is easier to push down the growing distress when I notice certain truths about that myself. I still drink too much, I am still too pliable, too nice. I still believe this was my fault. I still feel nauseous when I hear your name. I am still afraid of sex. You still do not know you raped me, I still cannot say that you raped me.

A meta-analysis of 28 different studies on females aged 14 and over who had experienced non-consensual sex through force, threat or incapacitation found that 60% of these women did not acknowledge that they had been raped.

However, as Zoe Peterson, a clinical psychologist who leads Indiana University's Kinsey Institute Sexual Assault Research Initiative, says "it's really important to be clear that whether or not someone labels a sexual assault or rape as a sexual assault or rape, it doesn't necessarily influence whether or not it's traumatic"

Our brains natural response to terrible or traumatic incidents can very often be denial. Therefore it makes sense that so many people find comfort in believing what happened wasn't rape.

Assaults are very frequently minimized by being called cases of 'miscommunication' or 'bad sex'. It has been thought that not acknowledging rape may aid in protecting people from absorbing the stigma that is associated with rape.

Alcohol also plays a huge role in how a victim and others view a sexual assault, despite the law clearly stating that a person who is heavily intoxicated cannot consent we still see a lot more reluctance to disclose an incident if a person was drinking whilst a sexual assault occurred.

Psychotherapist Richie Sadlier and psychologist Elaine Byrne teach a module in sexual health to transition year students in a school in Ireland. In one class they were focusing on consent and alcohol – the responses from the young men ranged from 'You could ask them straight out if they're up for it' to 'That's fucked up! So if you go out and you both get drunk you can't have sex? Isn't that, like, 90% of how people have sex in Ireland? Get drunk first and then shag?"

There were disagreements on whether slurring words was to be considered too drunk or not or if falling around would be an indicator of being too drunk but "that happens to everyone too'

> At the end of the class the students were asked "if you were asked to explain consent to someone now, what would you say?" The response – "I'd tell them to never drink and stay a virgin cause it's not worth the fucking hassle"

Female, 20

I was fourteen when I had my first experience of sexual assault. It's a memory that only popped into my head recently as if I had been suppressing it for all these years. My cousin threw a house party for his twenty first. Everything was so new to me at the time; it was probably my first time being at a party with alcohol and drugs. I remember getting ready, with no expectations for the night other than what I had seen from American coming of age movies and episodes of Skins. I put on a black dress from New Look and was so excited to pretend I was an adult for the night. Me and my cousins would sneak cans and bottles of wine upstairs and choke on cigarettes in the hope that we even slightly resembled the 20-something year olds passing through the party. The alcohol took over at about 1 o'clock and I decided to call it a night and passed out in the single bed in the spare room. Things were blurry at this stage, the room was dark and I saw the door open and light coming in from the hallway. The door shut again and the sounds of chatter and music disappeared. A silhouette of a man stood in front of me. He started talking and I immediately recognised his voice. It was a man I had been talking to earlier on in the night. I remember fancying him solely on the basis that he was older and paying me attention. He was in his mid-twenties and had brown eyes and looking back was clearly on drugs. When you're that young and naive and so desperately pretending to be older you don't see the problem with that age gap. I just felt mature and attractive. He sat down beside me and asked my age. I told him I was 16. Up until recently I would beat myself up for the lies I had told and the way I behaved but how was I supposed to know anything. I had no experience with the world. I looked 14 and my abuser knew it. He was taking advantage of me. He started to rub my leg as I sat there on the bed. I began to feel really uncomfortable but was too afraid to say anything. I didn't want to embarrass myself or come off as "uptight". All I could think of was telling my friends the next day and how cool I would seem to have gotten with a twenty year old guy. He made his way up my leg and kissed me and did what he wanted. I started to physically shake, my body's way of telling me that this needed to stop. But it didn't. He kept going until he got bored and left the room. I didn't sleep that night. I blamed myself and thought that I was prudish. It had to be my problem right? How could I possibly not enjoy this experience with an older man? I was a child and looking back now I can say that I was sexually assaulted. I never saw the man again and he probably never thought of the situation again. Who knows how many people he took advantage of. I was abused in a vulnerable situation and left to process my emotions alone - causing me to have a strange relationship with sex for years after. I've had a number of similar encounters since that night. I've helped friends go through similar encounters too. There is nothing good about sexual assault. No silver lining, no learning, nothing. The only thing I will say is don't be afraid to speak out about the abuse you've experienced. You'd be surprised at the amount of people who have lived through something similar. Supports are there, people are here to listen.

Female, 22

When I was 19 my three older cousins and I got a hotel room in the city so that we could have a girls weekend. One of my cousins brought one of their close male friends from university who was 25 at the time. This person was someone I was familiar with and my family knew and trusted (let's call him Ben).

Anyways, like any other normal night out we pre drank at the hotel and then went out into the city. This was my first time going out with these cousins so we were excited. They were buying me a lot of drinks. We were having fun. My cousins and I were dancing. Ben was meeting and talking to other girls and dancing with us but I didn't think he was being flirtatious or sexual with me in any way at this point.

My cousins, as they were older, decided they wanted to go back to the hotel. I wasn't ready to go home yet. I wanted to dance more and get some food - I stayed out with Ben as I felt safe with him and like I could trust him. And like I said he hadn't been coming onto me in any shape or form.

From there on it gets a little hazy.

I have no recollection of getting back to the hotel. I remember being confused about the layout of the room though and feeling as though something was off. I noticed it was the same but different and none of my things were here. I was heavily relying on Ben to stand up. While I had a lot to drink it wasn't any more than I would usually have on a night out - I later found out that he had drugged me using Flunitrazepam.

I remember him lifting me and putting me on the bed. I remember being cold and saying no but I have honestly blocked out a lot of what happened from that point onwards as this is how I deal with grief or trauma. Previously when I crashed my car I didn't initially remember the crash until months later when I experienced what felt like the same movement in the car as had been in the crash.

In the morning I woke up completely undressed and I couldn't find my clothing. I went to the bathroom wrapped in a sheet. I called my cousin and sent her my location. I found out that I was actually in the same hotel building, down the hall from my original room that I was meant to stay in with my cousins.

My cousins asked management if there was a room under my name or his name. They gave them the room number due to the circumstances.

When they found me two of my cousins took me back to their room still wrapped in a sheet. My cousin who's friend he was went into the room where I had left him sleeping and confronted him. They no longer talk or have any contact.

I have not seen him since and did not have sex for two and a half years as a result.

Bits and pieces come back to me now still during intercourse and this often deters me and prevents me from having sex with someone; especially if they do not know the circumstances and things that I have experienced.

> *Flunitrazepam is a powerful hypnotic drug. It has powerful hypnotic, sedative, and skeletal muscle relaxant properties. The drug is sometimes used as a date rape drug.*
>
> *There has been very little concrete evidence into how often date rape or drug facilitated sexual assault (DFSA) occurs as research has been difficult to gather. This can be due to the lack of services for people to check if they have been drugged, reluctance in coming forward due to a fear of judgment or belief that they may have taken the drug willingly and also the fact that the victim may not feel ready to come forward or disclose immediately.*
>
> *But DSFA does not just refer to someone being drugged without their knowledge. It also includes a perpetrator taking advantage of the fact*

that a person has taken drugs or alcohol and is incapacitated due to this.

A survey of 1'053 college students concluded that 9% of women who had been sexually assaulted suspected they had been drugged immediately beforehand.

The self-reports of rapists also align with those of victims. A clinical psychologist called David Lisak conducted a survey of 1'882 male college students who's sexual activities met the criteria for rape but had not been charged with assault. The results showed that 81% of these men reported that they had sex with women who were incapacitated due to alcohol or drugs. It was not specified in the survey if they men had caused this incapacitation or if they had preyed on these women as they knew they were incapacitated. Assaulting women under the influence of alcohol or drugs is by far the most common method used for sexual assault – only 9% of rapists reported to have used threat or force for sexual intercourse.

With cases like the above it's also so important to remember the fact that most perpetrators are not strangers. They are the people we know and as said above, the people we think we can trust.

Female, 21

For me I have experienced mostly sexual harassment. Especially at night time on the streets I have experienced groups of older drunken men yelling at me when it is dark and I just needed to speed walk to the closest lit and busy street. I feel almost every female I know has had a moment like this and that is just not okay.

. . .

Also in Paris a man actually followed me for a block on his scooter without me noticing - I only realised when he came up behind me trying to talk to me! I was near home and there were people around so I wasn't too scared but if I had been far from home I would have been terrified. It was so creepy he was older, around forty years old and he kept staring and it was scary how I didn't notice when I usually think I'm observant.

Female, 24

In September 2019, everyone in my college course was returning to campus after having been on Erasmus for the previous year. None of us had seen each other in so long, we were all so excited to get together for catch-up cans. My friends Damien, Stephen and myself sat on a bench in college for hours and hours the Tuesday evening of that Fresher's Week, yarning about everything we had missed in each other's lives. We retired to Damien's on-campus accommodation when security told us it was too late to stay on the bench, and we spent another few hours there, sitting, chatting, and laughing until our bellies hurt. We ran out of cans at about 10pm, but kept on talking, slowly but surely sobering up.

At about 12:15am I realised I needed to go if I was going to make the last LUAS home. We still had so much to chat about, so Stephen offered to let me sleep at his apartment just off Dorset St., walking distance, instead of rushing to get the public transport to mine. I didn't think twice, agreed, and we stayed chatting for another while. Some-time after 1am we wrapped it up, and Stephen and I started heading for home. Everything was completely normal, conversation was flowing, and we were getting fairly sober by this point. We arrived in his apartment and watched YouTube vibes on the TV while we drank some tea, and talked even more. When it was finally time for bed, I asked if I could a T-shirt to sleep in, and he offered me his favourite Morrissey merch (in hindsight, a red flag lol).

I asked if he had a blanket so I could crash on the couch. He said he actually didn't have a blanket, and that maybe it would be easier if I just shared his double bed with him. The thought of this made me a little bit uncomfortable, but not in the sense that I worried anything would happen without my consent- it was just that I thought he might make a move on me, and I would have to let him down gently, and it might make things awkward. My discomfort was based in awkwardness of slightly wounded feelings, not at all in fear. After all, I had been friends with this man for years now, we had maintained a long distance friendship from different countries... it didn't occur to me that he would do anything wrong.

What choice did I have, already in his apartment at 2am, but to agree. We climbed into his bed, him on the left against the wall, me on the right nearer the door. We watched YouTube videos on his phone until finally I rolled over onto my right side, facing away from him, and fell asleep.

I don't know what time it was when I woke up, but it was still dark out. I was still on my right side, facing the door, so I couldn't see him. I heard a noise. A repeating noise. A quick paced noise coming from under the covers on his side. I froze in my spot, facing the door but barely able to see at all, as I realised he was masturbating. I was in shock, as the noise got faster, and faster, and sloppier, until finally he let out a moan and a shudder. I was so careful to seem like I was still sound asleep. My eyes were wide open, wondering if I was dreaming it, trying to make myself believe I was dreaming it.

He did not get up to clean himself up, he rolled over and slept in his mess.

I lay awake, trying to think rationally. Obviously I wanted to get up and simply run away as fast as my legs could carry me, but that couldn't have made sense, for a number of reasons. My phone was on the other side of the room, near dead. I didn't have money for a taxi, and it was too early in the morning for the LUAS to be running. I didn't even confidently know my way from his apartment towards town. I couldn't get up and bolt, I would have to get dressed, put my shoes on, find my coat in the living room, and figure out how to get out of his building. Surely some part of that would wake him up. And I thought, if he's out of his mind enough to have done that, who knows what else he's capable of doing right now?

So I lay there. Like a statue. For god knows how long, pretending to be asleep, on my right side, eyes wide open.

As soon as the sun came up and I could hear distant LUAS bells, I got up, dressed, and got all my stuff together, fast enough that I don't even really remember doing it now. I said 'right I'm off, thanks for having me!', trying not to let on that I knew what he did, in case he'd do anything else. Much to my dismay, he got up to hug me goodbye. He held onto to the hug for a little bit too long, and I could feel bile rise in my throat. He unlocked the door and let me go, and I finally got on my LUAS home, desperately wishing I had done that at 12:15 the night before.

. . .

In the aftermath, I was so conflicted about what to do. This man had been my friend, and was very much a part of a circle of mutual friends. I knew that I didn't want to have to be around him ever again, but was it wrong of me to expect the rest of the friend group to avoid him with me? I decided to go ahead and tell the female members of the group what had happened, just so that they wouldn't find themselves in the same position, as I knew I would feel even worse if I never told them my story and then they fell victim to the same. This was the right decision to make. Not only because I felt better that my honesty might protect them, but also because they could not have been more supportive, considerate and deeply empathetic if they tried. I don't know what I would've done if not for them. Over the following few days, they stayed with me all the time in college, so that I'd never find myself alone in a corridor with Stephen. They helped me to work through what had happened, make sense of it, and regularly reminded me that what had happened was not my fault.

In terms of confronting Stephen, I mulled over my options for a while. He's had a history of mental health issues and suicide attempts, and I was worried that if I told him that I never wanted to see him again because of what he did, that he'd end his life, and I would have to live with that guilt. It was almost like I was trying to balance the line between respecting my own instincts (never wanting to see him again) with trying to respect him. I don't know why I felt the need to show him respect when he had so blatantly disrespected me. I guess I had some sort of moral high ground complex, as if I was trying to figure out what was 'objectively' the right thing to, so that nothing would come back to haunt me? I didn't know what to say to him or how to say it- it seemed like a serious enough conversation to have privately and in person, but being alone in a room with him was obviously my absolute worst nightmare at this point.

What I eventually decided to do with Stephen was to send him a message, stating that I was awake for what he did to me, and that I did not wish to be in his company anymore. I told him that all I wanted was for him to get help for himself. Having been friends with him for so long, I knew he was capable of being such a wonderful man, and I wanted him to know that I believed he could get the help he needed and end up being a happy healthy person one day. To this day, I'm glad that my message was firm and assertive, but also rooted in the kindness and supportiveness that make up my personality. I believe that there is bravery in staying soft, and not letting adversity harden your spirit. I'm glad that I did not let Stephen's abuse of my good nature damage it.

His response to the message was deeply apologetic. He claimed that the combination of his new antidepressants, sleeping pills and alcohol makes him unaware of what he does while he sleeps, apparently he had been sleepwalking and finding himself in unexpected places. I don't know if I believe all of that, and even if it's true it's no excuse. He shouldn't have invited me to stay if he knew he couldn't control how he would behave.

Stephen dutifully stayed away from hanging out with our group of friends, and if he saw me in the library or sitting somewhere in college he would immediately turn around and go somewhere else. To be fair to him, he made it a little bit easier for me to try to forget the whole thing. I think he was sincerely ashamed.

. . .

I was able to process it all as I told my various friends what had happened, and they were all so kind to me, checking up on me, making sure I had company when I wanted it and time to myself when I needed it. At this point in my life I didn't have a counsellor or seek any kind of professional support, but luckily, in this specific case, I don't think I needed to. My wonderful loving feminist friends gave me the free therapy I needed, simply by giving me all the space I needed to talk about it, and I didn't get traumatised by the event. I'm over it.

Months after the fact, I ended up telling my rural Irish mother, and she responded exactly as I knew she would: initially empathetic, but slowly fading into the classic narrative of 'boys will be boys'. She claimed I walked myself into the situation, and that I should've known that men can't control themselves. I rolled my eyes as she spouted these patriarchal scapegoats she had been raised on, and was glad that I had waited until after I was already over the whole ordeal to tell her. She meant well of course, she's not a bad mother by any stretch of the imagination, she's just a woman that grew up in the 60's and 70's. Not her fault.

Stephen graduated the following year, and was having drinks in Doyle's to celebrate. Our old mutual friend Richie called me from Doyle's, saying that I should join them for a drink as Stephen would be moving to China shortly afterwards. I told Richie that I didn't want to have a drink with Stephen, and Richie said 'ugh, don't you think it's time you forgive him?'.

The things I learned from this chapter in my life are as follows:

1. Be there for your friends in the same ways that you would want them to be there for you.
2. Focus on your own healing, don't listen to people second guessing you or suggesting it's 'time to forgive him'. They don't know your heart.
3. The LUAS is always there for you.

The Sexual Experiences Survey in 2020 – which was a nationwide survey of students in Ireland – asked 6000 students about their experiences with sexual violence and harassment. Over half of first year students had been sexually harassed since starting college.

This figure continued to rise as the years went on with it being 62% of second year students experiencing sexual harassment and 66% of third year and higher.

However the levels or reported harassment or assault are still so low.

In this survey just over 70% of respondents who had experienced sexual misconduct said they didn't know what happens when a student would report an incident – only 16% had received information on how to seek help and under 10% knew how to report an incident.

Sexual harassment and assault in college is a growing epidemic, and yes there is more education around consent than there used to be, but this means there is more awareness so we are only hearing more now than we used to. It may not be that it happened less years ago. It may be that women are finally feeling as though they will be heard when they speak.

It is also a problem that didn't have to exist when only males were allowed to go to college. In 1904 Trinity let its first females attend and that year there were less than 1000 students and only 40 of them were women.

Today there are 15'500 students and 8000 of them are women. It is a different world in college today than it was.

Consent education in college wasn't a number one priority when there were only males in college. Now there is more women than men in Trinity.

Adolescents and young adults are four times more likely to be victims of sexual assault than women in all other age groups. In the vast majority of these cases, the perpetrator is an acquaintance of the victim.

Female, 22

When I was away one time I was followed all the way back to my hotel by two men.

Another time I was punched after I told a man to fuck off because he was catcalling me and whistling at me….

One time I had to get my friend to help me get a boy out of our apartment because he was demanding sex.

My ass was slapped by a stranger in broad daylight in the middle of the city.

> *"I think it's worth saying that everybody knows a girl who was raped but nobody knows a rapist"*

Female, 21

I remember the day it started. The day my experience with sexual harassment became more than just a cautionary tale my mam had warned me about. I was fourteen years old, walking home alone in broad daylight from the St. Patrick's Day Parade. The car slowed down- full of men at least twice my age- honking and screaming at me, windows down. I was so embarrassed. Why me? After all, I was nothing to look at – I had barely hit puberty. But that didn't seem to matter to them.

After that, things escalated. Every house party or night out of my teenage years would consist of spending half the night avoiding the gaze of men ogling me and my friends, pressing up against us and breathing heavily down our necks, refusing to take the hint when we looked them in the eyes, asking them to leave us alone. The trek from the bars to the dancefloors involved weaving in and out of crowds of wandering hands, while keeping a close eye on my drink for fear that someone would slip something in and swoop in to be the "hero" when I inevitably pass out 20 minutes later en route to the taxi rank. I can't even count the number of times I had to link arms with one of my lad friends, asking them to pretend we were dating so the handsy men would go away. As if the only reason they should stop grabbing my arse was because I had a boyfriend and not solely because I had asked them not to. My words meant nothing until they fell from the lips of another male. It seemed that bro code went deeper than any respect they had for me or my friends.

I got to thinking, maybe this is just an Irish thing? Surely men in other countries are a bit more respectful? "It can't get much worse than here", So I was only delighted to be granted the opportunity to study abroad. A chance to experience nights out for six months straight where I could just dance with my friends and maybe even- God above imagine- be able to leave my drink down unattended for thirty seconds!

· · ·

I couldn't have been more wrong.

Not a single day passed where I left my apartment to walk to university or visit the supermarket less than a minute away without having to pass a group of men, all laughing and sneering, who would just so happen to stop talking as I walked past, their voices falling silent as their eyes stopped to scan me from top to bottom. I glanced in the rear-view mirrors of parked cars along the curb, staring them down from a safe distance as they egged each other on to make comments about my leggings or my top or my collarbones peeking through. I could never do anything but that- stare at them and curse them out of it from a safe distance- after all, there were six of them and one of me and I had heard of brave women fighting back and not living to tell the tale.

I endeavoured to make a 15-hour bus journey from my Erasmus city to visit my friends on holiday two countries over. I was a broke student who missed her friends from back home and plane tickets cost a fortune, so what choice did I have? I also remember talking to my friend who was concerned about my voyage and saying something along the lines of, "what's the worst that could happen on a bus?" It's not like it was going to be like the busy trams where every man cops a feel before fading back into the throngs of commuters before you can identify the culprit. However, it turns out that I didn't even need to be in a crowd or around a gang of men to feel scared, unsafe and uncomfortable. It took only one.

I was the last pick-up along the bus route, and much to my dismay, all of the seats were filled bar one. I remember scanning the seats, hoping and praying for a seat beside a friendly looking old woman or even a girl my age, but no. The only seat was beside a man who noticed my predicament and was beaming at me. I walked over, nodded my hello so as not to be rude, and took my seat, turning my earphones up full volume, signalling in the most polite way possible: please take the hint that I just want to sleep. Almost immediately, he turns to me and speaks. My eyes snap open and I take out an earphone. "Pardon?" I said, as he repeated his question. "What's your name?" A million thoughts crossed my mind and the lessons of stranger danger from my primary school days rang through. I gave him the first random name that came to mind. This appeased him and he smiled again. I sheepishly smiled back and went to put my earphone back in. For the love of God man it's late, let a girl sleep!

Then came the onslaught of questions, each more creepy and personal than the one before. It began with questions like "where are you from?" "Why are you here in France?" before reaching the real nitty gritty- "is your boyfriend meeting you when the bus reaches the destination?" Alarm bells were ringing in my head. Why was he trying to suss out if I was going to be alone? I spun some story about how my "boyfriend" was going to be collecting me from the bus station, yes of course. There was another lull in the conversation so I made another attempt to put my earphone back in. Wrong move. He copped the ring on my finger- the middle one on the left hand- and grabbed it. "Are you engaged? Are you married to this boyfriend?" I shook my head, in shock that my hand was now in his. He smirked then- clearly I should have said I was married- and he started complimenting me.

It first started as "you have nice hair…. Your eyes are so green….. Your foreign accent is nice to listen to", before it escalated. He started to hold and squeeze my hand, interlacing my fingers with his despite the fact that my hand was frozen solid in fear. Surely the fact I'm not reciprocating should be indication enough that this is not okay? Then his hand slipped down to my knee as he stared out the window, a massive grin on his face, while I felt sick to my stomach glancing down at his hand violating my leg wondering how I was ever going to get away. There were still thirteen hours of the journey left after all.

His hand slowly inched its way further up my leg, until his hand was resting on the horizontal part of my seatbelt lying across my lower stomach, far too high up for my liking. He fell asleep like that. I was frozen with fear, glancing around to see if anyone had noticed what had transpired. No one even blinked an eye. I sat completely still wrestling with my thoughts: do I fall asleep and hope I wake before he does so he doesn't put his hands beneath the seatbelt? Do I try to move or would that be misconstrued as an invitation? My thoughts raced back and forth for hours, my brain exhausted but too stressed and scared to shut off for even a moment.

Suddenly. A glimmer of hope. The driver said something in a language I didn't understand before the bus engine stopped. The man startled, removing his hand from where it didn't belong in the first place, and explained, "we're taking a pit stop in this petrol station". Freedom! I ran off the bus, all my belongings in tow, and sprinted to the bathroom of the dingy petrol station, locking myself into the cubicle. I felt so unclean and alone. There was an entire melting pot of languages and cultures on the bus and I didn't recognise a single one. How could I ask someone to switch seats with me like this? Even if I could, was it immoral for me to subject another person to sit beside this man for the remainder of the journey? How could I tell him I was uncomfortable and didn't want to speak to him for the rest of the trip without making him so mad that he hurts or threatens me? I came up completely short.

I glanced at myself in the mirror. Maybe it's what I'm wearing? I took my hoodie off and tied it around my waist, hoping the sleeves would act as a further deterrent to my upper thigh, and that the knot would stop him trying to slip his hand beneath the seatbelt. I clambered back on to the bus and he was already sitting back in his seat. Great. I put my earphones in again and decided to put my bag on the rack above my head. Maybe if I had more leg room, I could extend my legs and then he couldn't touch me with such ease. I reached up with the bag and felt his eyes snap back to me. My top had come out from beneath the knot of my jumper, exposing half an inch of my stomach. His hungry eyes filled with glee and he smiled the most disgusting smile. I felt awful and sick to my stomach, stuffing my top back underneath as fast as my shaky hands could manage. I plonked myself down, avoiding all eye contact with him. He rummaged around in his bag, revealing a bag of sweets. "Have one", he urged. My voice shaky feebly replied, "no, thank you". He pressed on, shoving the bag closer to my face while he inched ever closer to me. Steely-eyed I stared at him and said, "I said no, thank you". He was aghast, and I was shocked as to where this force had come from. He sat back in his seat, leaning away from me and staring out the window, arms crossed like a child having a tantrum. I was momentarily relieved- I had finally stood up for myself! But then my thoughts took a dark turn. You've angered him now, and who knows what he'll do, now scorned, his masculinity in tatters.

I stared down at my phone screen for the rest of the journey, although it was the early hours of the morning and no one was on the other end. Any time he stirred, my heart lurched, scared he'd strike and I'd get my comeuppance for being so brash before. He could literally do anything to me, I thought, and no one on this packed bus would notice or even care. Soon enough, we had another pit stop and once again, I fled the bus. It was nearly noon now and I finally had Wi-Fi from the bus station. I frantically texted my family group chat, briefly describing what was happening but trying to convince them I was okay and in control of the situation- a major white lie- knowing that they'd be concerned but were unable to help from 1000 miles away. The driver beckoned us back onto the bus. I only had three more hours left to go. I could do this.

All was forgiven with the man it seemed, though, as he waited for me by the doors of the bus to get on. He was beaming at me and chatting incessantly about God-knows-what. He ushered me onto the bus, insisting I walk before him up the bus steps. I tried to protest- "you're sitting beside the window it makes sense you go in first"- but to no avail. I could feel his eyes burning into my bum at his eye-level as I climbed the stairs. Humiliating. But what could I do?

He somehow seemed to get the gist that I was in no mood for talking for the next few hours. Peace at last. Until there wasn't. We were gradually coming into the final throes of our journey when his questions picked up again. "Where did your boyfriend say he was going to meet you in the bus station?" Panic gripped my body. I had never been to this country before, I didn't know the first thing about the station. What do I tell him? "At the bathrooms", I blurted. "And what does he look like, this boyfriend of yours? Do you have photos?" I was properly freaking out now. There was no boyfriend, I had made that up hours ago. So what was going to happen to me when we pulled up and this non-existent boy was not going to be standing at the bathrooms with open arms waiting for me? "Ehm, sure. Give me a second, I want to find a nice one", I said, as my brain went into overdrive. Aiming my phone screen away from his view, I desperately turned on my 4G, praying that for the first time on this entire trip, I would have some sort of signal on the bus. Someone was looking down on me. One bar. That'll do. A flood of messages and missed calls came in from my family, begging for updates to know that, since my last message, I was okay. I texted in, "finally have internet, someone call me quick".

He probed, "well? Where's this picture?" "Sorry", I grimaced, "my internet is being really slow". Then the noise I'd been waiting for, my phone rang. I answered so fast I nearly cracked my screen and my dad's voice came through the other end, asking me a million questions a minute. I explained in Irish- the only language I could speak that I was certain the man couldn't understand- that I could only answer in yes or no format as he was listening to every word I was saying, trying to catch me in a lie. Dad and I chatted for the remainder of the trip, strategically planning my swift exit from this nightmare. I heard the voice over the bus intercom stating the name of my stop. This was it. The bus grinded to a halt and Dad on the other end said, "run".

I unbuckled my seatbelt so fast, grabbed my bag from the rack and took the stairs two at a time. Luckily, as I was last on, my suitcase was the first to come out from the hold of the bus. I grabbed it and ran so fast the wheels barely touched the ground. Bathrooms were right in front of me but that's where he would expect me to go. That's where he would want me to go. That's where he would wait for me. I kept running with Dad on the other end of the phone racking up a fortune on his phone bill. I found another set of toilets further down and flung myself into one of the cubicles. My legs were like jelly, hands shaky, face as pale as a sheet. I finally had stronger signal to turn the call into a FaceTime, tears streaming down my face. With Dad on the other end, I eventually gathered enough courage to walk back through the station, my eyes darting back and forth constantly, scared the man would appear from around a corner and call me out on the lack of a boyfriend at my side. Thankfully, it seemed as though I had had a lucky escape and eventually made it to the hostel where my friends were staying, tired and anxious but grateful to have survived relatively unscathed.

I wish I could say that that was the last time that something along those lines had happened, but alas; no. That was nearly two years ago now, and if anything, that day on the bus has made me more aware of the dangers that lurk in the most mundane of places. Simply going for a walk around my hometown with my best friend or walking home from the train station late at night or in the comfort of my university gym- nowhere is safe from the piercing gaze and feelings of un- comfort akin to those I felt on the bus that day. And I am not alone in this- all of my friends have similar stories to tell.

This cannot continue. We must do better.

> *"We don't fight for our own happy endings. We fight to say you can't. We fight for accountability. We fight to establish precedent. We fight because we pray we'll be the last ones to feel this kind of pain."* —
> *Chanel Miller, Know My Name*

References

https://www.verywellmind.com/sexual-assault-and-victim-blaming-4802707

https://www.thejournal.ie/sex-consent-survey-3102174-Nov2016/

https://www.irishtimes.com/life-and-style/health-family/everything-you-want-to-know-about-consent-but-were-afraid-to-ask-1.3450246

https://www.thejournal.ie/myths-sexual-violence-4850444-Oct2019/

http://thebrief.muls.org/sexual-harassment-in-clubs-and-bars

https://www.bbc.com/future/article/20181102-why-dont-rape-and-sexual-assault-victims-come-forward

https://www.irishtimes.com/life-and-style/health-family/so-if-you-go-out-and-both-get-drunk-you-can-t-have-sex-that-s-f-ked-up-1.3840294

https://www.bbc.com/future/article/20181102-why-dont-rape-and-sexual-assault-victims-come-forward

https://www.irishtimes.com/life-and-style/health-family/so-if-you-go-out-and-both-get-drunk-you-can-t-have-sex-that-s-f-ked-up-1.3840294

https://www.irishpost.com/news/survey-reveals-many-college-students-in-ireland-not-reporting-sexual-assault-187390

https://www.irishtimes.com/news/women-s-hour-at-trinity-1.1134451#:~:text=Today%20there%20are%2015%2C500%20students%2C%20more%20than%208%2C000%20of%20them%20women.

https://pubmed.ncbi.nlm.nih.gov/9806126/#:~:text=Results%3A%20Lifetime%20prevalence%20of%20-date,high%20of%2068%25%20among%20adolescents.

The cover of Her Word is a painting by Katie Whelan, an artist from Cork who paints with the Crawford Supported Artist CIT.

Support Services

- Women's Aid National Freephone Helpline 1800 341 900 – This is open 24 hours a day, 7 days a week

- National Rape Crisis Helpline 1800 778 888 which is operated by the Dublin Rape Crisis Centre and open 24 hours a day, 7 days a week.

- **One in Four** – Support and resources for people who have experienced sexual abuse and/or sexual violence - (01) 662 4070

Acknowledgments

Writing Her Word has been one of the most ever-changing, emotional, challenging and most importantly, rewarding experiences of my life. It has continued to surprise me, people have continued to surprise and inspire me, my characters have continued to surprise and challenge me.

Her Word took a form that I had not expected at all. From the moment I started to collect real people's stories it seemed as though that was the real truth to Her Word, that this was the real reason I was writing this book. Often, when we start writing, we do not know why. I started Her Word when I was 18, and many title changes, years, long stops, impulsive starts, words and chapters later we are here, and I know why.

I believe that Bill, a character and writer in one of my favorite movies "Stuck in Love" puts it perfectly. He says - 'that's what writing is – it's listening to that beating heart, and when we hear it, it's our job to decipher it to the best of our abilities'

A novel is born from hearing a beating heart that grabs us, from hearing or seeing something that sparks something so strong in us that we can't not start to search, learn, ask and most importantly, type.

The very first person I want to thank is you. Thank you so much for picking up this book, for reading it and if you make it to the end, thank you.

Her Word would not exist without so many of you. I know that many of you who are reading this book are in here within the pages, that many of your stories, your bravery, your very own personal experiences are kept within these very sentences. For that I am so grateful, and I truly believe so many other people are so grateful for it too.

I also want to thank my amazing cousin Katie whose beautiful artwork is the cover of Her Word and who has the ability to spread so much laughter and joy to whomever she meets.

My amazing family, my kind and inspiring mum, my supportive and adventurous dad, thank you both for always allowing me to be me.

Thank you to Eamon who is never not supportive, to Kylie who has always been so caring.

To my siblings - Tom, Harry and Phoebe. You have all always supported all of my ideas and endeavors. I am one of the luckiest girls in the world to have so many family members to call when I get good news. Regardless of time zones and distances.

And to my cousins, who are like siblings to me, Eoinie and Caoimhz, thank you for making family be people and not a place, as long as we are together.

To my JJ, it might be a different book and a completely different time in our lives', but you're support, love and absolute kindness never ever changes. Neither does our friendship, thank you so much for being my person. Love you, obviously.

I want to express so much gratitude to my Spring Chicks, Aobhoo, Becca, Pippa and Sash. There are very simply no words that would be near good enough to thank each of you for making our years together the most loving, supportive and incredible. For making every day an adventure. For making every night a story to tell. You are all the most incredible women and I feel so blessed every single day to wake up surrounded by you all. The book of our memories and mishaps is pending ladies.

To my Figs, together there is absolutely nothing we can't do. Thank you for supporting me, for making me laugh, for showing me love and family and making me feel like no matter what happens, we will always be much more than okay.

To my Hots, many, many years later we are still here, and we still have the capability to make each other laugh till we cry, even if now it is glasses of wine in our hands and not hot chocolate.

To my other amazing and incredible friends, Aoife C, thank you so much for being the most encouraging and kind woman. Being with you is always a reminder in how kind humans can be. Tara, thank you so much for always being there through all the years of our madness, for laughs and spontaneity. To Rachel K, thank you for being such a loving, funny and caring human.

I have had the privilege of working in different social care and hospital settings that has allowed me to meet some of the most inspirational and determined people. I am so grateful to so many of you for opening my eyes and teaching me so many things about this world.

To Stephanie and the team at Red Penguin, thank you so much for being the most encouraging and enthusiastic team to work with. Your passion for what you do, for words and stories made me want to make Her Word the very best version of itself. Thank you so much.

And as always, thank you to life. To chance and circumstance, for me being here today. Thank you to everyone who has passed through my life and is in my life, who has made it what it is today. I don't know what I did to deserve a life that is so filled with love and happiness, but I am so grateful for it and for all of you.

About the Author

Izzy Hodder is a 22 year old Mental Health Nursing student in Trinity College Dublin. When she's not writing or at college, Izzy spends her time teaching yoga, swimming in the sea and dancing. Izzy's main loves in life include people, manifesting and booking one way flights. *Her Word* is Izzy's second novel.

www.ingramcontent.com/pod-product-compliance
Lightning Source LLC
Chambersburg PA
CBHW071956070526
44583CB00015B/1218